W9-BGX-839

EVER WESTWARD THE LAND

Anna Maria Foxwell James, 1806–1879, a photograph taken in the early 1870s, by courtesy of David James

EVER WESTWARD THE LAND

Samuel James and his
Cornish Family on the
trail to Oregon and
the Pacific North-West
1842–52

by

A. C. Todd with David James

UNIVERSITY OF EXETER

First published 1986 by the
University of Exeter

ISBN 0 85989 233 6

The University of Exeter is pleased
to acknowledge the generous contribution
of Mr David James towards the
printing costs of this book.

Exeter University Publications
Reed Hall,
Streatham Drive,
Exeter EX4 4QR
United Kingdom

Printed in Great Britain by A. Wheaton & Co. Ltd, Exeter

To our Helpmates

Edna and Maria

THE AUTHOR

Dr A. C. Todd was Resident Tutor for West Cornwall in the Department of Extra-Mural Studies of the University of Exeter from 1947 to 1969. He was, *inter alia*, a Fulbright Fellow at Berkeley and Visiting Professor at the University of Arizona. As well as several other books on Cornish and American history his publications include *The Cornish Miner in America*, Truro, 1967.

CONTENTS

MAPS AND ILLUSTRATIONS

MAPS

ILLUSTRATIONS

Preface

Historical accounts of the emigration of the Cornish to North America in the nineteenth century have been dominated usually by the exploits of metal miners and the export of their expertise and technology. Little attention has been showered on the exodus of farmers and indeed scant notice seems to have been taken of them at the time of their departure. Generally it was unemployment, hunger and sheer destitution which drove the miners away and denuded the towns and villages of the best of their young folk. For a miner to seek his fortune abroad was not unusual and departures from the main railway stations were an almost everyday occurrence. Farmers, hardly ever faced with such severe economic deprivations, were pulled by, rather than pushed to, the United States for reasons other than lack of money to buy food. Their reasons for leaving Cornwall seem to have been complex but generally to do with dissatisfaction with the state of the country and its leaders, both in Church and State.

At least that is the conclusion reached from a study of a group of farmers who in the 1840s left the Helston and Lizard areas for Wisconsin. Among them were Samuel James, his wife Anna Maria and their four sons, the eldest being only eight years old. Their original intention was to settle in Wisconsin among relatives, but some inner restlessness urged Samuel to pioneer ever westwards to the very end of the Oregon Trail and then beyond to Puget Sound, a feat of endurance, courage and resolution excelled perhaps by no other Cornish family, especially as he was then middle-aged. There he founded the settlement that bears his name, Jamestown, which to this day remains a colony of descendants whose ties with Cornwall have grown even closer with the passage of time.

Samuel James agonised for some time over the wisdom of abandoning Cornwall for the young American republic and exposing his family to the harshness and risks of journeying into the unknown, perhaps dying thousands of miles from where they were born. Miners left Cornwall in the belief and hope that they would return rich to invest in mines near where they had always lived, but farmers emigrated in the expectation never to return, for poverty was hardly a compelling factor. Indeed Samuel owned valuable property and so was not attracted by free land in America. The truth was that he and his relatives and their friends were yeomen farmers, many of them owners of freehold land. They belonged to a sturdy and independent class who considered that their hard-won freedoms were being eroded by governments in which their interests were not represented. Rather than surrender they were prepared to sell their land in Cornwall and start a new life in the United States where their qualities would be appreciated. Samuel was bitterly critical of governments which imposed taxes for wars he did not agree with, and of churches, both Anglican and Methodist, which irritated him on account of their bureaucratic control. And he was more than a match for his opponents for he was remarkably well-informed and of a studious turn of mind through his reading of newspapers like the *West Briton* and the *Sherborne Mercury* and his comprehensive library.

But, as well as being a practical farmer and a realist in the affairs of the world, Samuel was also a romantic idealist who cherished a vision of the United States as a youthful vigorous farming republic where it was possible to rediscover for oneself a spiritual fulfilment. He was searching for a land, he said, where 'the light of Heaven, the vital air, the fish of the sea and the produce of the earth necessary for the sustenance of man are free for all as intended by their great Creator'.

Strengthened by a forthright certainty that God lives first in the hearts of men and women, and that a 'church' exists when even only two or three are gathered together and anywhere, Samuel and Anna Maria began their search for a new home. It was also to be a spiritual journey, a quest for a place where God dwelt. Symbolically that meant a daily dying unto oneself on the trail that led ever westwards into the dying sun in the sure expectation of a renewal of strength and purpose with its rising on the morrow. Through their experience of each day's battle for survival across deserts and over mountains they rediscovered each other and knew that when at last they saw the Pacific Ocean their pilgrimage was at an end. In Washington Territory, six thousand miles from Cornwall's Atlantic Ocean, Samuel lived out his useful life, making his voice heard as an abolitionist in the great debate on the negro slavery problem, counselling the local Indians on their rights against white predators, and tending his land and cattle. His influence on his descendants has been immense. Annual family gatherings, which began in the early 1900s, continue to this day. 'To-ings and fro-ings' between Seattle and St Keverne in Cornwall are almost an annual occurrence.

Over the years family enthusiasts, and especially Samuel's great-grandson, David James, have discovered and carefully preserved letters and other documents of their revered ancestor. Of these, the most important is the terse 14-page working journal that Samuel logged when crossing the plains in 1851, together with the rough topographical maps he sketched on the way. The journal was deposited in the library of the University of Washington at Seattle in the 1930s but has been missing for many years. Photocopies may, however, be seen in the Pacific North-West Collection of the University of Washington and in the Oregon Historical Society (MS 1508–MISCL: *Overland Journeys to the Pacific*). The photocopies were fortunately made by Albert V. Shephard, a grandson of Samuel James, when he was curator of the North Central Washington Museum at Wenatchee and researching for his book, *Migration of a Family*. This was privately printed in 1941 and a copy was presented to the Special Collections of the Washington Historical Society at Tacoma.

Twenty letters of Samuel James have also survived. They cover the years 1840 to 1866 and deal with such matters as conditions in Cornwall, Wisconsin, Oregon and Washington Territory. One long letter of 1860, addressed to John Thomas of Predannack, Mullion, was published in *The West Briton* of 3 August 1860, and deals solely with advice and encouragement for Cornish men and women who wished to emigrate to the United States. The originals of these letters are in the possession of David James of Bainbridge Island, Washington, and Mr and Mrs Thomas Foxwell of Elgin, Iowa. Copies may be consulted in the Special Collections of the Washington Historical Society, 315 North Stadium Way, Tacoma, Washington 98403. For Samuel's views on matters of public interest and concern, there are the letters and articles he wrote for local newspapers about farm life and fruit production (signing himself as 'Plowboy'), slavery and the Free Soil Movement. They are to be found in *The Columbian* of 25 January, 25 June, 12 and 19 November, 1853; and in *The Pioneer and Democrat* of 26 August, 2 September, 25 November 1854, and of 5 May, 1 and 8 June, 1855. Runs of these Olympia newspapers are available in the Pacific North-West Collections of the University of Washington. Finally, for Samuel's views on religion there exists an important manuscript document of some thirty pages in the County Record Office, Truro, Cornwall.

Three other significant primary sources of information need to be mentioned. First, there are three letters from his wife, Anna Maria, to relatives in Cornwall and Wisconsin, dated 1852, 1866 and 1870. Copies of these are with the Washington State Historical Society. Secondly, there is the journal of Mary Ann Frances James Shephard (1848–1912). Two years before she died Samuel's daughter set to work to write her recollections of her pioneer days in Oregon and Washington, but as she was barely three years old when she was taken over the Oregon Trail she leaned heavily on her father's journal to jog her memory for the details of that part of her life. The manuscript has not been published and is now held by a great-granddaughter of Samuel, Mrs Ronald Mitchell of Seattle. Lastly and rather more reliable are the extensive reminiscences of Mary Ann's brother, John Rogers James, who was born in Cornwall in 1840 and had reached the impressionable age of ten when his father's wagons rolled out of Wisconsin. His autobiography, 35 pages long and written in 1916, was published in Volume 2 of a series entitled *Told by The Pioneers*, which the USA Federal Public Works Administration commissioned in 1938. A colourful personality, John Rogers was recognised as a reputable historian of the Oregon Trail and was much in demand after 1910 as a lecturer on the subject when a new generation began to appreciate the influence of the trails to the West on the development of the American character, and especially those who came under the influence of Jackson Turner and his concept of the American frontier. Several short accounts he wrote on pioneer life in Washington Territory and State have not yet been published. They remain in manuscript in the possession of his great-nephew, part author of this book.

David James is today's family historian and the curator of all existing James material. A journalist by profession and lately a Director of Washington State Historical Society, his admirable book *From Grand Mound to Scatter Creek* (Olympia, Washington, 1980 and 1981) is the starting point for any subsequent studies of his quite extraordinary Cornish family. Without his diligence, enthusiasm and constant encouragement, laced together by his frequent visits to Cornwall, *Ever Westward the Land*, to which he has contributed chapters 9–12 and much information about the others, could not have been written.

Both authors wish to put on record the help they received from the late Dr Alton Moyle of Madison, Wisconsin, and Thomas Foxwell of Elgin, Iowa, both of whom have their roots in the same part of Cornwall from whence came Samuel James, and who made frequent pilgrimages there. For guidance on the Oregon Trail section of the book they are indebted to Clyde Arbuckle, former city historian of San José, California, who has walked many a mile of the trails to the West and demonstrated to coach-loads of enthusiasts the art of becoming trail-wise. They are grateful too for the assistance of the following in Cornwall: Mrs Esther Johns of Porthleven; Mr F. L. Harris, OBE, MA; Ivor Thomas of Carbis Bay; the Revd Thomas Shaw, formerly of St Keverne; the Nicholls family of Trelan, St Keverne and the staff of the Cornwall County Record Office, Truro. They acknowledge with thanks the courtesy and cooperation of the staff of the British Library and Museum in London; and finally the University of Exeter, the Publications Officer and her staff, and Professor Joyce Youings, who made valuable suggestions to improve the presentation of their work.

A. C. Todd

Leamington Spa
February 1986

CHAPTER 1

Leaving Cornwall in 1842

SAMUEL JAMES, a stout and heavily built Cornishman, whose large head, deep-set eyes, dark hair and heavy eye-brows gave him a look of authority and assurance, was born in 1805. He was the son of a yeoman farmer, from whom he eventually inherited a farm called Chywoon comprising five hundred acres of arable land and the imposing granite family house of Trelan (built in the 1700s and still occupied) in the parish of St Keverne on the edge of Goonhilly Downs. These downs are a part of the southern Cornish peninsula known as the Lizard, a bleak moorland of browns and greys except in springtime when it is aflame with the green and gold of the gorse against the blue of the sky. In 1835 Samuel was cutting a road near the southern edge of the downs. He unearthed several graves in one of which he found a rare Bronze Age mirror, which can now be seen in the British Museum and is known as the 'St Keverne Mirror'. But for many a seafarer the Lizard has been his first, and perhaps last, glimpse of England, for its cliffs enclose a graveyard for ships. Today the holiday-maker from 'up-country' is perhaps more enchanted by the silvered sand of its many coves and beaches and intrigued by the concave dishes of the English Post Office earth station which in 1962 picked up the first television pictures from the United States. This however was not the first link between that country and this corner of Cornwall. More than a hundred years earlier the then young American republic was being talked about by many a Cornish farmer, fisherman and metal miner, as they wrestled with the problems of economic depression and wondered what new hopes might await them on the other side of the Atlantic.

From his father Samuel inherited not only valuable material possessions but also qualities of a special kind that were to be a significant factor, as they were for others, in compelling him to emigrate to the United States. The gravestone in St Keverne churchyard which he erected in memory of his father describes him as a 'yeoman', and so was his son. It was a word that denoted pride and respect for a set of particular social values and attitudes. The 'yeomen of England' were not gentry or squirearchy, still less great landowners. They were not distinguished by armorial bearings, family crests or titles. They were, however, the proud owners and occupiers of land which they and their forbears had acquired through their own initiative and industriousness, compact farms, hedged with thornbush or, as in Cornwall, with dry-stone walls. They also helped to improve the standard of life of the landless by employing them. As their consolidation of land ownership increased so did their influence. Yeomen sat on juries and some even became magistrates, responsible for maintaining order and settling local disputes. Rooted in the soil and its moral and ethical assumptions—'whatever a man sows that shall he also reap'—yeomen were comparatively well-educated, some of them at local grammar schools and then in a continuous way at home. Efficient farmers and sound businessmen, they were highly respected for their personal discipline and independence of mind. But in rural areas they contributed so much to the running of the country that they became a threat to the position and power of the gentry and the great landowners, already growing richer through their financial and commercial enterprises in India and the West Indies. As a result, from about 1700 onwards the yeomen farmers of England were on the retreat and their numbers declined as the more powerful landowners began to buy them out or edge them out by enclosing land through Acts of Parliament. Some showed their resilience either by becoming richer landowners themselves or by drifting to the towns where they indulged with varying success in managing new businesses.

But in Cornwall there was a different result. As most of the fertile land, always scarce, had already been enclosed and developed, new enclosures in the eighteenth century invariably consisted of waste and marginal land. So the small yeoman was not eliminated. On the contrary the number of smallholders of freehold land actually increased. But even so a new menace threatened the older and more established yeomen and their traditional qualities of independence and initiative. These, many a Cornish yeoman complained, were being chipped away by the policies of successive governments, so much so that they were even prepared to sell their farms and emigrate to the United States, where, they believed, their special gifts and qualities would be appreciated. Thus the Cornish yeoman emigrant was an unusual one. He had land to sell in order to buy land in America, where he was likely to become a most successful farmer because the traditional qualities he possessed were exactly those needed to make a successful pioneer for the opening up of the American farming frontier. Samuel James was even more unusual: not only was he more studious than most but he crossed the plains to Oregon and Washington Territory when he was already forty-five years old.

Saddened and frustrated, Samuel had watched many of his relatives and best friends, the Foxwells, the Moyles, and the Shephards, all yeomen farmers like himself, sell their land and board an emigrant ship at Falmouth to face the discomforts of an Atlantic crossing and make new homes and lives in Wisconsin, some by farming, some by lead mining, and many by both. Indeed he had

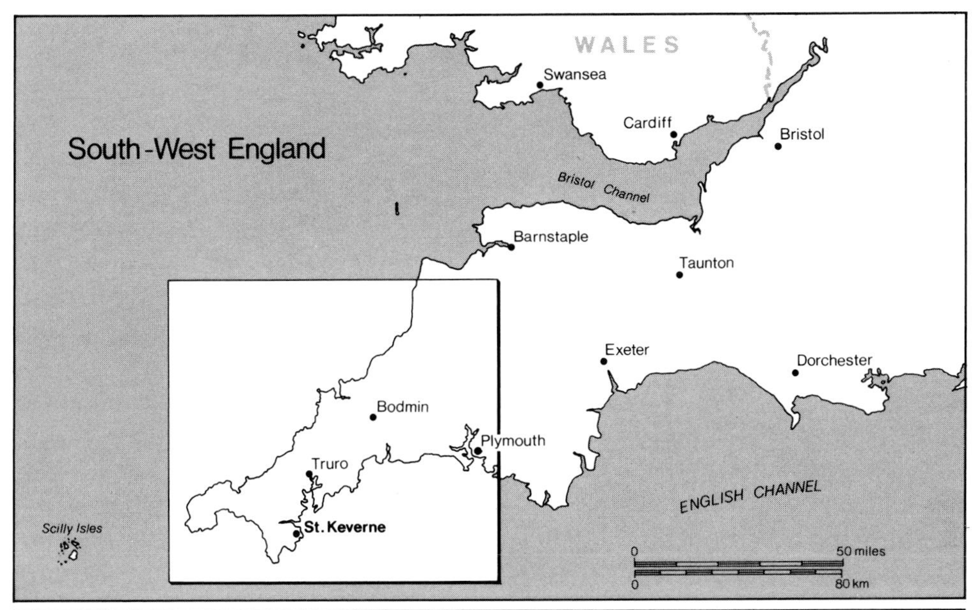
South-West England
WALES
Swansea
Cardiff
Bristol
Bristol Channel
Barnstaple
Taunton
Exeter
Dorchester
Bodmin
Plymouth
Truro
St. Keverne
ENGLISH CHANNEL
Scilly Isles
0
50 miles
0
80 km

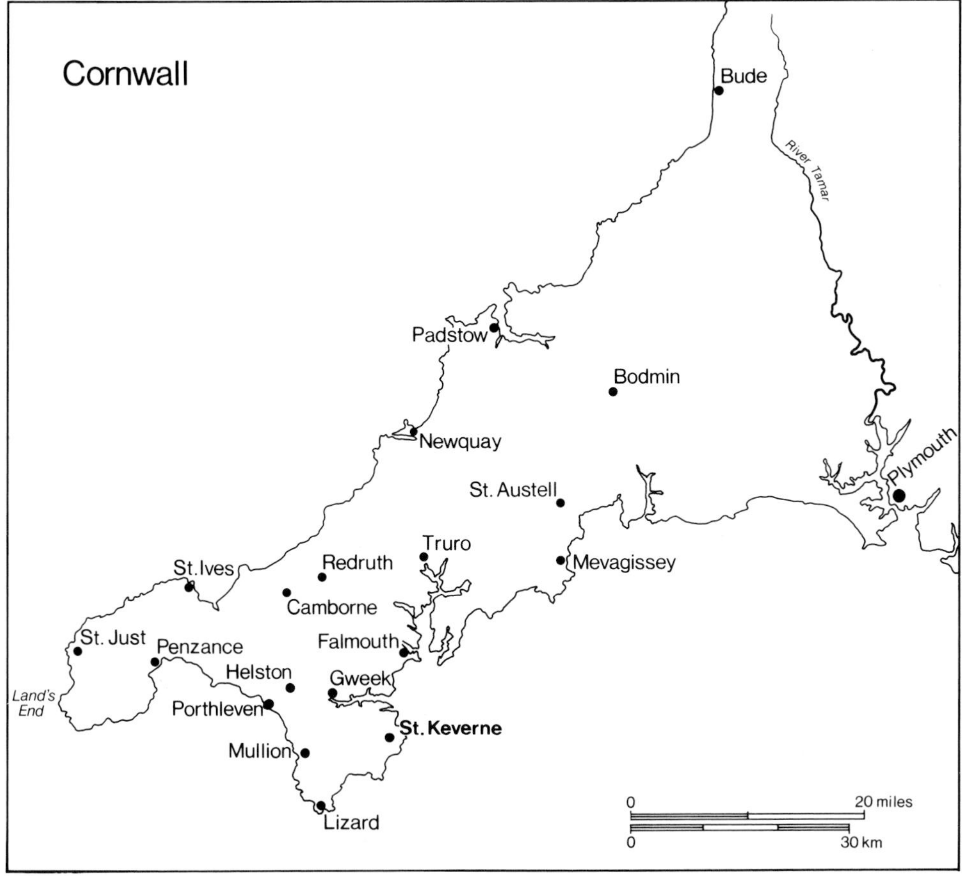
Cornwall
Bude
River Tamar
Padstow
Bodmin
Newquay
Plymouth
St. Austell
Truro
Redruth
Mevagissey
St. Ives
Camborne
St. Just
Penzance
Falmouth
Helston
Gweek
Land's End
Porthleven
St. Keverne
Mullion
Lizard
0
20 miles
0
30 km

married a Foxwell, Anna Maria, the daughter of an influential local Methodist preacher, William Foxwell. Born in Mullion she was a slim fair-haired girl of 'very pleasing address', who had received, according to her son, 'a thorough training in a young ladies' school' and could readily quote passages from the Bible and the English poets.[1] Her son John Rogers remembered her quoting passages from Gray, Wordsworth, and Pope when the occasion required. When his brother Tom wanted to work in a shipping establishment their mother was fond of reminding the family of Pope's lines from his *Ode to Solitude*: 'Happy the man whose wish and care/A few paternal acres bound;/Content to breathe his native air/In his own ground.' By the time her several brothers and sisters and her mother had decided to abandon Cornwall, she had produced four sons, Samuel, Thomas, William and John Rogers; and it seems that it was only a question of time before she and her husband would decide to follow.

The immediate reasons for their going were complex. After the end of the French wars, farming was everywhere depressed and especially so in Cornwall. During the siege economy, when English ports were blockaded, marginal land had been ploughed and seeded at high prices to encourage more food production while the more fertile areas had been racked year after year by sowing them for grain crops until the land was exhausted. This practice of artificial over-production continued in peace time even though it resulted in a catastrophic fall in prices. Farmers in Cornwall tried to ride out the slump by employing casual labour, hiring pauper adults from the dreaded workhouses, and even pauper children as farm apprentices, which depressed adult wages still further.[2] In addition farmers had to pay not only tithe to the clergy of the established church but also heavy rates to maintain the unemployed poor, as well as more general taxes to sustain in power a government of whose policies they did not approve. In 1822 there was a County Meeting at Bodmin where landowners and farmers denounced government extravagance, demanded a reduction in the level of taxation which would enable tithes and rents to be reduced too, and petitioned for Parliament to be reformed so that sinecure offices could be abolished.[3]

A short period of general prosperity followed but in 1829 a series of bad harvests brought all the old problems to the fore again, culminating in another meeting of radicals at Bodmin in 1831 with the usual demands for tithe, rate and tax reductions. In 1832 the extension of the right to vote in parliamentary elections did something to appease the reformers but the Cornish farmers still felt the need to campaign vigorously against the imposition of tithe, arguing that it deprived the poor of employment by preventing the improvement of waste land. Though the Tithe Commutation Act of 1836 defused discontent, Cornish farmers continued to claim, with some justification, that the new Poor Law placed increasing burdens on the rate-payers who had to provide workhouses on a district basis to house the unemployed poor.[4]

Samuel's daughter, Mary Ann Frances Shephard, describes how her father found himself trapped in the net of these economic policies, but she also mentions irritations of a religious kind. The Foxwell and James families were Methodists who repudiated not only the Church of England and its tithe, which served to keep Anglican squires in power, but also the episcopal nature of early Methodism. They considered themselves the purest of Wesleyans, renouncing hierarchies of any kind. Samuel himself was reared in the severest of Methodist traditions, according to standards set by his father-in-law William Foxwell (1761–1837) who, it has been said, 'altered the course of Methodism on the western side of the Lizard peninsula'.[5] William Foxwell, owner of five farms, was entirely self-taught, as he had to be at a time when there were few schools in Cornwall, and appears to have been a natural student, consuming every branch of knowledge that came his way and excited his imagination, especially astronomy, music, Greek, Latin, botany and mathematics. It was not long before he was chosen to be a local preacher and leader in the weekly Bible class which all committed Methodists were obliged to attend.[6]

It was in this class that Samuel sat and continued his education with the tools he had inherited from his father, a superb collection of books, to which he was to add many more. This library was so important and valuable to him that, when he emigrated to America, he freighted it across the Atlantic to Wisconsin and then hauled it in a covered wagon every mile of the long journey to Oregon and beyond—a dead weight of about 800 lbs. In his old age his son, John Rogers, remembered some of the titles of these books: Plutarch's *Lives*; the *Essays* of Sir Francis Bacon; John Locke's *Essay Concerning the Human Understanding*; Aesop's *Fables*; Cervantes' *Don Quixote*; and a 'number of books on travel and history'. There were several volumes about religion including a Greek New Testament, a Bible Commentary, a life of John Wesley, a history of Christianity, and Joseph Butler's *Analogy of Religion, Natural and Revealed, in the Constitution of Nature*. Other works included farming and cattle raising, as well as the poems of Goldsmith, Gray, Cowper and Wordsworth.[7] One forgotten collection (discovered by David James) was a two-volume set of *The Geographical Magazine or New System of Geography* by William Frederick Martyn, published in 1793.

But the most prized acquisition consisted of 25 volumes of *The Encyclopaedia Londinensis or Universal Dictionary of Arts, Sciences and Literature*, 'compiled, digested and arranged' by John Wilkes, 'assisted by eminent scholars of the English, Scotch and Irish universities'. The complete set is now housed in the State Capital Museum at Olympia, Washington, on permanent loan from the James family. It includes three volumes of copper-plate engravings illustrating 'the most curious, rare and elegant productions of Nature, in every part of the Universe, and enriched with portraits of eminent and learned personages in all ages of the world'. These engravings were to fascinate the Indians of the Pacific North-West and were to be a useful means of promoting friendships between them and the intruding immigrants.

For Samuel, as for Thomas Carlyle, a university is a collection of books, and so it was for his class leader and father-in-law, William Foxwell. They fuelled both his religious zeal and his dissent. When Foxwell died in March 1837, Samuel wrote a moving appreciation of him in the July, August and September 1838 editions of the *Wesleyan Methodist Association Magazine*. He described his wife's father as a religious reformer who was opposed to all authority in religious matters but that of the Holy Scriptures and the human conscience. Both he and Foxwell were even critical of the Methodist Conference in its assumption that it was the source of all power in the circuits and chapels through its insistence that no preacher could practice without its approval, thereby depriving the 'people' of their 'natural rights'.[8] Therefore they both became members of the radical movement that was launched in Sheffield in 1834, the breakaway Wesleyan Methodist Association. Known as Associationists, their numbers grew in Mullion and the Lizard from 54 in 1836 to 122 in 1839.[9] They found it increasingly difficult to live harmoniously with traditional Methodists and almost naturally found themselves the hard core of the emigration movement from the entire Lizard area in the 1840s, producing almost a second wave of Pilgrim Fathers. These Cornish pilgrims, like the first bearers of the name, are an example of a practical radicalism reacting against the establishment of the day, but in their case enriched by a new philosophy of non-conformity in religion.

The essence of that philosophy is contained in a document of some thirty pages written by Samuel James, perhaps after finally settling down in Washington Territory.[10] He begins: 'I take a church to be, in the first instance, two or three met together in the name of Christ, i.e. the church that is in thy house. Secondly, I take all the members of the church to be standing on an equality.' Here he is affirming what has been rediscovered recently, the ancient view of the Church as *Koinonia*, that is the local Christian fellowship gathered around a natural local leader, a bishop or elder who, according to Samuel, 'should be as well and thoroughly acquainted with all the members and their spiritual condition as a father with his family'. No one person, he maintains, in the early days of the Christian Church forced men and women to join a church. They 'came of their own accord' and furthermore 'met in any place where they could or they deemed suitable—in their own houses, in upper rooms, in hired houses, on the sea shore, on the banks of rivers, without ceremony, dedication or consecration.' There is one passage that must have been written for consumption in Washington Territory, where Samuel enjoyed a reputation as a 'Free Soiler' and abolitionist: 'Be careful of entertaining and countenancing wicked prejudice respecting the colour or race of man. These are the groundwork for slavery and oppression, especially in the case of Negroes and Indians, resulting not infrequently in bloodshed and wars.' So he urged all ministers and pastors to be 'forward in teaching your hearers that mankind are all brethren, that God hath made *of one blood* all nations of men for to dwell upon all the face of the earth—Acts XVII, 26.'

Ministers and pastors were of course essential, thought Samuel, but their powers ought to be limited. Therefore 'no one on earth shall be set up as Father or Master or Lord or Prince or Head or Chief or Bishop to exercise dominion and authority' because 'all members are brethren and equals.' Titles like 'Reverend' and 'Right Reverend' he abominated as examples of impropriety, sinfulness and blasphemy. Samuel's daughter sums up thus: 'These things, together with the glowing reports of opportunities which were everywhere offered with a lavish hand, made them turn to the Great Republic of the West for the future, as they preferred a democratic form of government to a monarchical'.

The 'glowing reports' came from Samuel's brother-in-law, John Foxwell, who had already made a successful landfall in Wisconsin in 1840, was living in Ohio, and was now urging his brother Thomas and their sister Anna Maria to follow with her husband Samuel and their family. A third brother, William, who had followed a different route and was farming at Columbia in Texas, was trying to persuade the entire Foxwell family to make for Texas where, by becoming Texan citizens, they could claim an entitlement to 320 acres of land. All this we learn from a letter which Anna Maria wrote to her brother John on 26 June 1840.[11] In it she scorns the whole idea of moving to Texas and concentrates on the necessity of leaving Cornwall for Wisconsin because:

> Instead of happy England, it is become since you left much more unhappy and there are at this time hundreds and thousands of families in Cornwall alone who have not more than half food. All kinds of food is high and labour slack. The coming crops appear to be nearly destroyed in many places by the drouth. Farmers cannot afford to employ and many mines are stopped.

Therefore at last, she happily reports, her husband, 'Mr J. has lifted a foot in order to make a step in advance towards emigrating.' So, since she is 'bound to honour and obey, having long since formed the resolution of going where he goes and staying where he stays', she archly asks her brother some practical questions that might not have occurred to her husband:

1. Does the appearance of the inhabitants strike you as not being equally robust and hardy with those of our native clime?
2. Do you think the cares and anxieties of those who have emigrated with families are less than they might have been had they stayed at home?
3. Are cleared estates or nearly such so easily found as has been represented?
4. Could a farmer support his family and pay the outgoings on an estate of 200 acres freehold as comfortably as he could in England? You know our views of comfort and convenience.
5. Could a man, wife and family having a thousand pounds lay it out safely so as to be able to live on the interest of it in happy indolence?
6. Is a regular routine of farming as laborious as in England?
7. Is the scenery as beautiful as we have seen it described?
8. Are the beauties of the United States equal to the British fair who whirl about in omnibuses?[12]
9. What kind of Furniture should we bring from England to suit the American mansions?

10. Which are to be preferred—American *Helps* or English *Servants*—does not the character which the *Helper* prides himself on maintaining more than equal the trouble which is caused by the indifference and selfishness of our *Servants?*

She received an answer on 23 September according to a letter which she and Samuel jointly wrote to John on 17 October, composing alternate sections as the mood took them.[13] Anna Maria, after describing John's letter as arriving 'from the land of promise to us in the House of Bondage', revealed that on the first of September, 'I added a fine boy to our number to whom in consequence of a promise obtained previous to his birth we have given the name of John Rogers.' He was the boy who in late life was to write his autobiography, drawing on his memories of crossing the plains when he was 11 years old. Samuel, in a bantering mood, suggested that they had named him after a local celebrity who had written a pamphlet heatedly attacking popery, but in doing so 'chanced to grase [*sic*] (the most sensitive of all organs) the right eye of our glorious constitution—*the sacred established Mother Church*—and with the same lack of a certain kind of prudence suffered some of his random shots to light on the humble and devoted *helpmeet* of that sacred body, the Immaculate Wesleyan Conference'. They therefore proposed to give John Rogers the nickname of 'Antipopopriestian', to remind them of their dislike of all ecclesiastical hierarchies.

In the same light-hearted tone that soon turned to more serious matters, Samuel continued: 'We behold you [John] roaming at large in all the pride of independence or lolling at ease like *King Log* upon his throne, calling no man your master, while we are here racking our brains, racking our limbs, racking our lands in order to make them turn to more account than the Creator ever intended them for.' And for this state of affairs he blamed the Government and its foreign policy:

> The great European Powers are very jealous of each other on Eastern affairs. A battle has been recently fought at Beyrout, a city of Syria under the dominion of the Pacha [*sic*] of Egypt. The city was bombarded by the English fleet under Capt'n Napier and in a short time was reduced to a heap of ruins. Ten men on the English side were killed and upwards of 1000 dead bodies of the enemy were found among the ruins . . . France threatens to uphold the Pacha. The truth is Russia, England and France are trying to outgeneral each other and obtain possession of the East . . . In consequence of our warlike attitude we have a fresh accession of taxes. All the assessed taxes are raised 10% and the probability is further impositions must take place. Sugar and tea are raised greatly in price, the coarsest brown sugar being 10d per 1b. which happens to be a bad thing for the sweet lipped folks.

And to make matters worse, he went on: 'The smallpox has been every where [*sic*] among us [and] many have died, the greater number I believe through the maltreatment they receive. At the commencement of the disease the Doctors bleed them and there is scarcely one who is so treated that recovers.'

Thus there was every reason why they should make arrangements for leaving Cornwall now that John's letter 'has more than confirmed us in the opinion that you are gone to a better country'. But no final decision could yet be made because there had occurred a sudden demand for marl, which Samuel could scarcely ignore because a valuable and plentiful supply was available on his property. From May to October, he explained, he sold two thousand cartloads at sixpence a load, which brought him a useful profit of £50, buyers coming from Mawgan, Constantine, Cury and Manaccan for the rich clay which would improve their poor soils. The marl, said Samuel, was 'so promising a Spec[ulation] . . . that Emigration thoughts for the present we fear must stand aloof as far as we are concerned.' There were, however, other compensations for, in the digging of the marl-pit, Samuel had unearthed 'the remains of an ancient burial place' of human bones, earthen urns, copper and brass ornaments and 'two rings, one broken and one entire about the size of an umbrella ring, another about 3 inches in circumference and the thickness of a goose quill which by its weight and colour is judged to be gold'. Anna Maria jokingly observed that her 'poor husband has been troubled with golden dreams.'

However, by the end of 1840 Samuel had at least made up his mind why he wanted to emigrate, even though the timing still had to be determined. In a remarkable letter to John Foxwell of 12 December 1840 he tabulates with some warmth twelve reasons:

1. To escape the heavy charges of supporting *certain useless institutions* [by which he means the Anglican Church, Parliament, the Methodist Conference and even perhaps the monarchy of the new and young Queen Victoria].
2. To escape from supporting a State religion which in Tithes, Church rates etc. acquires 1/5 at least of the landed produce of the Kingdom and is at the same time *worse* than useless—spiritual opium druggers.
3. To escape from the pressure of the enormous load of national debt, £800,000,000 which cramps and bars all rational improvement, prevents free trade and drains our pockets and no attempts are made to reduce it.
4. To avoid the horror that would attend war under the above circumstances.
5. To enable me to support myself and my family comfortably without its requiring all the energies of my body and mind.
6. To live under free and useful institutions in a country where taxes are almost nominal and where those which are paid are merely for conducting public business in an economical manner and for public instruction.
7. To live in a country and settle my family where there is the least probability of present or future wars.
8. To be where I hope to be most useful and to be able to assist those to emigrate who are otherwise unable.
9. To go where the light of heaven, the vital air, the fish of the sea and the produce of the earth, necessary for the sustenance of man, are free for all as intended by their Great Creator.
10. To go where industry reaps its own reward.
11. To avoid the painful scenes and supporting the abominable oppression of the Poor Law Bastilles.
12. To avoid having the trouble and difficulty of managing so many servants and so much business and so much property for overbearing despots who will bear no part of the loss attending it.

Here then was heard the voice of the true democrat arguing fiercely and convincingly against the oppression of the unnatural but established marriage between Church and State. Here Samuel was shouting for the rights of the hard-working and anxiety-ridden yeoman farmers who found themselves and their families crushed to the point of desperation by inept and time-serving politicians who could not solve the problems of unemployment and poverty except by forcing the unemployed into the Bastille-like workhouses and increasing rates and taxes to keep them out of work. Samuel desperately wanted to find refuge and strength in a country where his energies, integrity and industry would be recognised, encouraged and rewarded so that he could 'be most useful' in shaping a society where the value of a public system of education, lacking in Cornwall for most of the nineteenth century, was appreciated. His arguments gave a compelling power, especially where he feared being caught in another long period of war.

Samuel elaborated on this pacifist theme, warning John Foxwell of the dangers of the extension of British imperialism in the Far East: 'Our fleets and armies have made captures in China and have taken possession of the important island of Choushan which they intend to keep hereafter as a part of the British Empire.' He was to be mistaken about Choushan, one of a group of islands in Hangchow Bay, but correct about British ambitions in the South China seas. Palmerston's foreign policy had clearly alarmed him and indeed the occupation of Choushan had a wider significance than Samuel imagined. He had already referred to Anglican priests as spiritual opium druggers and it is conceivable that at the back of his mind was his worry about the English trade in opium, grown in India and then sold to Chinese merchants through the East India Company's factors, all of them making substantial profits. The effect of opium-smoking among the Chinese was so devastating that the Emperor appointed a special commissioner, Lin Tse-Hse, to stamp it out. His first move was to surround the British merchants operating from Canton at the mouth of the Pearl River and to order them to surrender their opium and themselves, though later they were allowed to seek refuge in the nearby Portuguese Macau.

Palmerston, in aggressive mood, decided on a policy of coercion—to force China either to agree to a new commercial treaty or to cede to Great Britain a small rocky island off the mainland where the British could carry on their opium smuggling unmolested. The island he had in mind was Hong Kong. In June 1840 he despatched a naval force to Hong Kong and another to Choushan. When Samuel was writing his letter a pattern of events was in train which was to lead in the following month, January 1841, to the Convention of Chuendi, by which China ceded Hong Kong to the British Crown. It seems quite remarkable that, feeling so strongly about foreign policy in the Far East, Samuel should have considered it as yet another compelling reason for leaving Cornwall. Not only, it seems, was he a man who, far from the heart of events in London, kept himself informed about current affairs, no doubt through his regular reading of the *Sherborne Mercury* and *West Briton*, but he was also perceptive enough to appreciate the significance of those events, for he foresaw the coming weakness of a country if it extended its external commitments too far for its security: 'The old lady Britain has brought forth a good many children and while she gives suck (tiddy) to them they may keep pretty close to her but the *weaning* time is the thing to try their willingness to support the old Lady's extravagances.' Indeed within the next hundred years the weaning time was almost over and the children were about to take off to pursue their own extravagances.

Samuel was in buoyant mood when he wrote that letter, looking forward to his family's arrival in 'the land of freedom' after escaping from 'the House of Bondage' because 'our bondage here is indeed more intolerable than ever.' At last he had made his decision and more or less figured out the time of departure: 'I must sell part or all of my estate before I can go and in consequence of that shall not be able to leave before May or June,' in which case he would be joined by the family of his brother-in-law, Hannibal Shephard. 'Hannibal and myself think of bringing out one dozen reap hooks, three or four scythes, some shovels and broad axes, gig harness and iron work for a gig, fowling pieces [i.e. guns], clock, watches, plough iron work, knives and forks, saddle and bridle, several yards of blanketing, garden seeds, Whittington wheat, a good sort for sheltered ground.' And he even thought of shipping to Wisconsin his 'large iron roller' for breaking the clods of earth after ploughing, but it weighed almost a third of a ton and presumably was left behind in Cornwall.

But it was not until the autumn of 1841 that the final and irrevocable decision was made. Writing again in a joint letter on 23 October to John Foxwell with some sighs of relief, Samuel refers to a previous letter from John which 'we could not but regard as something like a providential guide to our tottering steps. After considering and reconsidering the case and viewing it in all its phases and spending more time (I really believe) in conferring over the matter than would have put us to America we are at last coming to the determination and humbly hope for the Divine blessing on this most important step.'

Anna Maria reveals in the same letter that the day of decision was her birthday, 15 September. From now on she was all haste and excitement, asking her American cousins to send her 'a list of prices of the articles most used in common wearing apparel such as shirtings, calico prints, flannels, shoes, stockings', and questioning: 'What would you advise as to feathers and how can you get them?' Samuel, no less elated, is more concerned with the kind of land his brother-in-law should buy for them:

> I am at last determined by the Divine assistance to wind up my affairs here and set my face towards the land of promise. I should like to settle near you if possible on which account I would be willing to forego some qualities in an Estate which I would otherwise deem to be desirable. I should like if such might be obtainable to have a gently inclined surface with here and there a living spring, trees sufficient to graft and overcome old General Frost and with cheerful blaze drive him

> discomfited from our habitation. Let us hear from you immediately for what sum you can purchase and how we can remit to you the purchase money . . . Let me know what kind of a domicile that I may be guided in what to bring for it. When you look out through the windows is there anything between your face and the elements?

Passages to New York were booked on the emigrant ship the *Orient*, scheduled to sail from Falmouth on 4 April 1842. Even now the decision was a hard one because it meant Samuel and Anna Maria separating. For one thing, the sale of Trelan and the farms had not been completed (there were to be complications even after they left Wisconsin for Oregon) but, more importantly, Anna Maria, now 36 years old, was six months pregnant. After much heart-searching over changes of plan, it was finally agreed that she should go on ahead with the two youngest boys, Thomas aged three and John Rogers not yet two. Samuel and the two older boys, Samuel junior aged eight and William six, were to follow later. Fortunately Anna Maria would not be travelling alone. Other members of her closely knit family were emigrating too: her brother William, her sister Susan with her husband Thomas Moyle and their baby in arms, and her widowed mother. Ann Foxwell, though 60 years old, jokingly observed that she had no alternative but to leave Cornwall now that her husband was dead. She

Left: *Part of the Lizard Peninsula, Cornwall, April 1986, with the Lizard Point in the distance and in the foreground the present hamlet of Trelan.* Photograph by RNAS Culdrose. Above: *Trelan Farmhouse, St Keverne, Cornwall, 14 April 1986.* Photograph J. Youings

was William Foxwell's third wife and, as the family legend has it, as the previous two had been buried on either side of him, she certainly had no desire to be buried at his feet!

So the pregnant Mrs James was in safe hands and indeed among familiar Cornish faces. The passenger list of the *Orient* shows that 188 of those on board came from Redruth, Camborne and Helston and the villages around.[14] There were 73 families; 50 men classified as miners or farmers; 40 mothers; and 77 children, their ages ranging from two months upwards. One mother, Marie Cundy, was even more advanced in pregnancy than Anna Maria and was to give birth to a boy in mid-Atlantic. Naturally they were all apprehensive and Samuel knew the risks. Most of the passengers had never been aboard a ship before, even though they lived within sight of the sea. For a voyage of at least six weeks, they had to provide their own food, the captain being responsible only for the provision of water. It was not unknown for the cooking to be undertaken on the open deck. Samuel worried about the safety of the vessel, as well he might. It seemed barely seaworthy after many years of service carrying spices and silks, as its name implied, from the Orient, but its owners considered it still serviceable for its human cargo. Thomas Moyle, who kept a journal during the voyage,[15] records that the master, John Leuty, 'prayed long, loud and often on the way over, promising the Lord if He would save him this once more, he would never take the old tub to sea again'.

The crossing was a nightmare as the spring gales hit the *Orient*. 'Great valleys and trenches' opened in the sea, all took to their bunks in a dismal effort to ward off sea-sickness, no fires could be lit in the caboose, children whimpered with cold and hunger, the stench of vomit was everywhere, the foremast was smashed and swept overboard, ropes and rigging entangled the deck and water could not be rationed out until nightfall. Because the passengers were 'very much dissatisfied', according to Thomas Moyle, he preached them a sermon every day to remind them that God had 'prospered our way so far', but understandably they remained sullen and unconvinced. The captain summoned him to bleed the thumb of one of the crew and gave him 'a rusty lance' to do it, but Thomas preferred his own tools, those of the farrier. He even used them to extract 'a tooth from Miss Edwards'. Mrs Thomas of Camborne died, leaving a distraught husband and three bewildered children under the age of five to mourn her at the eventide funeral when the sails were furled and the ship hove-to. 'At 5 o'clock the body of her whose spirit had gone to glory was consigned to the great deep wrapped in canvas with two bags of ballast', wrote Thomas Moyle. Little had happened during the voyage to swell his belief that man was by nature good: 'Find every man's hand against his neighbour, and even friend if anything is to be got thereby. Every man serves his own and even when to the disadvantage of others.' It was now, when Whitsuntide was near, that he thought most of home: 'Thought much of Sunday School tea gathering. Would like to be with them. But satisfied with present prospects.'

Perhaps he was writing when the *Orient* was preparing to dock in New York on 19 May for by then the worst seemed over for the passengers. But Anna Maria's anxieties were as painful as ever as she wondered whether she would reach Wisconsin before her child was born. However, the overland route for the Cornish to their land of promise was, relatively speaking, idyllic: by steamer up the Hudson River to Albany; then by barge to Buffalo through apple country along the Erie Canal; from Buffalo over the lakes to Racine in Wisconsin; and finally by jolting wagon, surely not at all to the liking of Anna Maria, to their home destination of the village of Caledonia in Racine County. Her immediate gift to her new home was to endow it with a new life. On 26 July 1842 she gave birth to her first daughter, Anna Eliza.

NOTES

1. David James, *From Grand Mound to Scatter Creek* (Olympia, Washington, 1980), p. 46.
2. John Rowe, *Cornwall in the Age of the Industrial Revolution* (Liverpool University Press, 1953), p. 239.
3. Ibid., p. 245.
4. Ibid., p. 246.
5. Ivor Thomas, *Methodism in Mullion* (Mullion Methodist Centenary Publications, 1978), p. 25.
6. Ibid., p. 22.
7. Autobiography of John Rogers James (1916).
8. Thomas, p. 26.
9. Ibid., p. 50.
10. In the Cornwall Record Office, County Hall, Truro.
11. The letters quoted here and on the following pages are in the possession of Thomas and Margaret Foxwell of Elgin, Iowa, whom the authors wish to thank.
12. The use of the word 'omnibus' is an indication of the newspapers and periodicals read by Anna Maria rather than a reference to a public vehicle of that name whirling along the lanes of Cornwall in 1840. Omnibuses appeared first in Paris in 1828 and somewhat later in London. Their very existence, it seems, was still something of a sensation in West Cornwall in 1840.
13. The letter is addressed to John Foxwell, 'at Thomas Reeds Esq'r, Strongville, Cuyahoga County, Ohio, U.S. North America (via Liverpool and New York)'.
14. Passenger Lists of Vessels arriving at New York, 1820–97, in the National Archives and Record Service (1957–8), Washington, DC; Microfilm Publications, Microcopy No. 237 of Records Group 36 in the Records of the Bureau of Customs.
15. In the possession of the Moyle family, Madison, Wisconsin.

CHAPTER 2

Unsettled in Wisconsin

We do not know exactly when Anna Maria was reunited with Samuel and their two eldest sons, though it is likely to have been some time later in that summer of 1842. Their arrival in Caledonia must have been a joyous event, a reunion not only of wife and husband, of brothers and the new sister, but also with the Foxwell brothers and their other relatives from Cornwall, the Shephards, the Moyles and the Richardses, who together more or less comprised the settlement and village of Yorkville. All lent their advice, help and pioneer experience as Samuel set to work to improve the farm in Caledonia which he bought from a Mr Beardsley and named Beardsley Vale. The land was well watered by the Root River that flowed into Lake Michigan at Racine and on it he built his first log cabin.[1] Between his homestead and the lake ranged flat and thickly wooded country with numerous bog-holes, marshes and swamps, while to the north and west stretched the never-ending pitiless prairie, its monotony relieved by intervening strips of standing timber.

Samuel had no doubt thought he would be farming for the remainder of his life in Wisconsin but such was not to be the case. His stay there lasted only seven years and of these we know little apart from the regular increases in his family: Ann Eliza born in 1842; Richard Oregon in 1846; in 1848 Mary Ann Frances and her twin brother, Allen, who was to die out in Oregon in the winter of 1852–3. Of all the children it is John Rogers, fourth son and the first family historian, who has preserved some vivid memories of their schooldays and life generally in Wisconsin. The school consisted of one room only and was located on the main road from Milwaukee to Racine and Chicago. It could only be reached by crossing a bridge over the Root River, though there were occasions when attempts were made to wade across with consequent duckings and punishments of switchings across the calves of legs. John Rogers reckoned that he owed most of his education to his parents, which is hardly surprising. His questioning about the meaning and pronunciation of words was always answered by his father 'without looking up' from whatever he was doing and 'without hesitancy'. Samuel so encouraged him that at the age of nine he was reading *Don Quixote*, Aesop's *Fables* and Bunyan's *The Pilgrim's Progress*. The latter, he says, 'made a very strong impression on my mind and contributed to my conversion afterwards'. The Bible of course in those days was *the* core subject and here his mother had sound advice to offer, that 'it would take away my old heart and give me a new one.'

He remembered with affection the round of the seasons: springtime with its profusion of flowers and the quick budding and leafing of the trees, so many of them nut-bearing such as walnuts, butternuts, hickory and birch; and the bountiful fall of crab-apples, thorn apples, plums, wild grapes, strawberries and high bush blackberries, the like of which he had never known in Cornwall. Dessert apples, however, were scarce and had to be freighted across the lake from Michigan or Ohio but 'fine apples they were, scenting the whole room with their fragrance.' Samuel owned a maple grove. In the spring John Rogers helped his father to tap the trees for the sap. He would drive a gouge or chisel into a selected spot on the trunk and insert a small wooden spike into the cut, from which flowed the sap into a bucket held by John Rogers. When sufficient sap had been collected, it was boiled in a large iron kettle until it thickened, and was then made into maple sugar cakes, the consumption of which was described as 'a fine treat'.

Another treat that John Rogers remembered with some relish was grey squirrel pie, accounted a 'pioneer delicacy'. Baked in a large deep dish about the size of a milk pan and surmounted by a heavy crust with the animals' heads serving as an ornamental ring and their lower jaws resting on the rim of the dish, it was not unlike the Cornish starry-gazy pie, in which the heads of herrings peered through the crust and leered at their eaters. But for John Rogers the best fish in the world was the lake white fish, which he and his friends caught by cutting holes in the ice and spearing them, for the icy waters seemed to give the fish 'more vitality and flavour'. Fish, together with milk from dairy herds, bacon from the hogs and 'occasionally some beef animals' meant that usually there was plenty of food to eat though not to sell, for these commodities realised only low prices on the local market. Thus there was often a shortage of ready cash. Indeed in those early days, 'most of the cash available was that brought with them by the emigrants'. Fortunately the James family had also brought with them a good supply of clothing from Cornwall, enough to last them for years: corduroy trousers and jackets with a plentiful supply of brass buttons; smocks and frocks of a navy-blue drill; and high 'stove-pipe hats for Sundays or special gatherings'.

In 1849 Samuel surprised his relatives and friends by announcing that he was returning to Cornwall to complete the sale of his property there and would take with him Thomas, his third son, then ten years old. But apparently when he looked out again on the well-remembered fields, cliffs and sea he decided not to return to Wisconsin and wrote to his wife to pack their books in barrels and return with the children to Cornwall. But hard on this letter came another to say that he had changed his mind again, that he had completed the sale and had booked berths on a ship bound from Liverpool to New York.

Of this voyage one event has been remembered on account of its closeness to a family tragedy, only averted by the resourcefulness of Samuel. Apparently when young Thomas embarked he was already infected with smallpox, and when the symptoms were revealed, vomiting, high temperature and the eruption of the tell-tale rash, Samuel feared that only one fate awaited his son. His daughter describes what happened:

> Now father, who was a man of quick thought and courage remembered to have noticed that the first mate was badly marked by the same disease, so he called him outside and told him of the situation. He and father knew that if the crew and passengers were to get hold of the facts it would certainly be a case of Jonah minus the whale, so they agreed to shut my brother and father in my father's stateroom for a bad case of seasickness. The necessary waiting-on was done by the mate; father seemed immune as he did not take it. Before the ship reached port, Tom was well again and no one on board even knew how close was the call for a first-class mutiny and I need hardly say that no one else had the smallpox.

What was it that caused Samuel to change his mind and return to Wisconsin although he had now no intention of settling there permanently? John Rogers says that his parents had begun to detest Wisconsin on account of the extremes of climate, the children being continually plagued by ague and fevers. That being so, Cornwall must have appeared attractive once more, and there is some evidence that Anna Maria positively welcomed the possibility of returning home again. What she did not know was that her husband had already been fired with the notion of moving her, not three thousand miles eastwards, but three thousand miles westwards to the Pacific Coast. John Rogers reckons that the idea came to his father when they were in New York, his heart being stirred by the sight of a group of Cornish miners, dressed in blue smocks and singing a song about digging for gold in California. The story is probably fanciful and unlikely. Samuel would hardly have allowed himself to be lured to goldfields, for he was first and foremost a farmer. There is no evidence that he was even associated with Cornishmen who were trying to win a fortune in the lead mines of Wisconsin.

The reason for his radical change of plan probably lay in ideas which had been germinating in his mind since at least 1846 and which suddenly fell into place in 1849. The year 1846, described by Bernard de Voto as America's 'year of decision', seemed to be the very epitome of Manifest Destiny. The Mormons were on the move to their promised land in Utah, they had already marked out a trail across deserts and over mountains, and President Polk was eager and ready to drive the Mexicans out of California and the British out of Oregon. Samuel must have been excited as early as 1846 by these events and especially by the opening-up of the American West, for that was the year when his first son to be born out of Cornwall was baptised and the names he and Anna Maria chose were, significantly and symbolically, Richard Oregon. One can well imagine their relatives and friends wondering why Richard's second name was neither Cornwall nor Wisconsin. But in 1846 Oregon came to represent a possible new direction in their lives, though as yet more of a hope than a likely reality until that historic day of 13 August 1848 when Congress created the new public domain of Oregon Territory.

Oregon had for years been prime country for the trapping activities of the Hudson's Bay Company, which sold the beaver pelts to China, a trade in which the Americans joined, notably John Jacob Astor and his Pacific Fur Company. But the British and Canadian penetration of the area by establishing forts and agricultural settlements stocked with cattle for California, pigs from Hawaii and sheep from Canada, mainly through the presiding genius of John McLoughlin, was so successful that it seemed as if the north-west corner of the continent must inevitably become a further outpost of the British Empire.[2] Samuel was a voracious and discriminating reader and the revival of American interest in the region by a handful of enthusiastic and patriotic pioneers could hardly have escaped his eye. The exploits of Nathaniel J. Wyeth, who campaigned for the formation of a Joint Stock Trading Company to develop American interests in Oregon, no doubt appealed to the adventurous Cornishman and particularly when he read Wyeth's account of his first crossing of the continent, reaching the Columbia River, returning to Boston and then repeating his epic adventure in 1834.

But perhaps of equal importance to a man of Samuel's religious persuasion was the compelling idea that new souls could be won for God in Oregon by despatching missionaries to convert the Indians. It seems reasonably certain that he had read in the Methodist *Christian Advocate* the accounts of Jason Lee crossing the plains in 1834, the establishment of a mission in the Willamette Valley, and the appeal for funds by the Methodist Church to assist emigrants to work there.[3] All this was common news, and in the very year, 1843, that Samuel was settled in Wisconsin with his family, the first of the great migrations to Oregon was already under way; 1,000 men, women and children of all ages and more than 5,000 head of cattle, from Ohio, Indiana, Illinois, Kentucky and Tennessee. While Samuel was sod-busting and timber-felling in Wisconsin in 1844 and 1845, new hosts of pioneers were battling their way west to make the American presence in Oregon significant.

Samuel could hardly stand aside from a people on the move for he had already shown that he, too, was a restless wanderer. Official reports, guide books and personal accounts of the new America to the south of the Columbia River circulated widely in the east, and no doubt some of them found their way into Samuel's library. There were at least thirty printed accounts of the attractions of life in Oregon that he could have consulted,[4] but the only one of which there is any record in the Jameses' family journals is J. Quinn Thornton's *Oregon and California in 1848*, published in two volumes in 1849. According to Samuel's son, John Rogers, this was the book which finally resolved all his doubts. He says they were all thrilled by a single incident in which Thornton described how he was negotiating a cut-off across the Cascade Mountains when he and his party were trapped in a blizzard: 'The picture of Mr Thornton exhorting the people to be patient and have courage, with the snow falling all around them, and the huge forest trees, dark and sombre, made an impression which father never forgot.'

But there was more than a single episode in Thornton's book to excite them and send their imagination racing. He was *the* authority on Oregon for he made the journey overland three times, in 1846, 1847 and 1848. He described in vivid detail the ever-changing landscape on the trail itself, the dangers to be encountered, and how the hostile terrain could be mastered. But more importantly, he devoted twelve chapters to the magic and attractiveness of Oregon itself. 'Oregon is greatly superior to Upper California as an agricultural country,' Thornton declared. Its population amounted to only twelve thousand, most of them farmers but distinguished for their industry, temperance and their 'public and private virtue'. Portland, Oregon, was a small and beautiful village of one hundred settlers which displayed an air of neatness, thrift and industry. Oregon City's population was still less than a thousand, but it supported a newspaper, the *Oregon Spectator*, and a public library.

A land of forests of fir, pine, oak, aspen, poplars and alder, of wild lupins, red honeysuckle and wallflowers, with a climate that was mild and healthful and where grass grew all through the winter, Oregon's most fertile soil was to be found in the Willamette valley where settlers could harvest an abundance of apples, strawberries, cranberries, gooseberries and whortleberries. Fish abounded in its many rivers, salmon came in six varieties, and its bays and inlets were alive with sturgeon, cod, carp, flounders, perch, herring, eel, crab, clams and oysters. Finally, Thornton had described the mud of Oregon and this led Anna Maria to exclaim that 'where there was mud in winter, the climate would be something like the old home in Cornwall'.[5]

As soon as Samuel returned home to Beardsley Vale, it was clear that his mind was made up and that he intended to plan for the move west. This was to occupy him for almost two years, not too long a time if the continental crossing was to be achieved without loss of life, cattle and equipment. Both he and his wife realised that harsh decisions had to be made, not only the parting from friends, but for Anna Maria leaving her mother behind in Wisconsin in the certainty that they would never see each other again.

NOTES

1. John Rogers James (1840–1929), *Wisconsin Memories*. He wrote his boyhood memories between 1900 and 1916 while compiling the history of his family's journey to Oregon. They were republished in 1983 in a booklet *Family Stories* (which celebrated a Foxwell Reunion at Yorkville in June 1983), pp. 20–4.

2. Ray Allen Billington, *Westward Expansion: A History of the American Frontier* (MacMillan, New York, 1949), pp. 509–10.
3. Ibid., p. 515.
4. Among them were: Elijah White, *A Concise View of Oregon Territory* (Washington, 1846); Miss A. J. Allen, *Ten Years in Oregon* (Ithaca 1848); J. Dunn, *History of Oregon* (1844); Daniel Lee, *Ten Years in Oregon* (1844)—he was one of Oregon's first missionaries; E. W. Tucker, *History of Oregon* (1844); C. S. Nicolay, *The Oregon Territory* (1846); and Joel Palmer, *Journal of Travels over the Rocky Mountains to the Mouth of the Columbia River, 1845 and 1846* (Cincinnati, 1847).
5. Autobiography of John Rogers James (1916).

CHAPTER 3

First Preparations

The overland crossing was to be in two stages. The first was to be spent in carefully preparing for the longer and more dangerous second stage, the 2,100-mile journey over deserts, rivers and high mountain passes. Samuel therefore decided to spend the winter months of 1850–1 at the frontier town of Dudley in Iowa where he would be conveniently poised for an early start in the following spring. He calculated that 1851 would be a better year than either 1849 or 1850, both of which had been disastrous.[1] The exceptionally heavy migrations then to California had resulted in untold sickness and suffering on the trail: a shortage of fodder through over-grazing had wiped out cattle and cholera had depleted the ranks of their owners. Samuel, a restless man in his Cornish fashion, was unlikely to leave much to chance now that he had sold everything for the promise of a new life-style in the West. And events proved him correct, for 1851 turned out to be an 'off year' on the trail with fewer wagon trains and consequently an abundance of feed for the cattle. Heavy migration was resumed in 1852 and resulted in the familiar losses.

On 5 October 1850 Samuel and his family were ready for their westward adventure and their first objective of Dudley some 400 miles away. Their entire possessions were stowed away in three stout wagons of seasoned hardwood, each pulled by three yoke of oxen. Their walking wealth comprised 'loose cattle' (cows to take the place of any oxen which dropped dead on the trail), three working horses and ponies for the children. Samuel later sold the horses and bought extra oxen when he learned that horses did not stand up to the rigours of the trail so well as oxen. Horses were nervous creatures, needed special forage, were soon exhausted and were a constant temptation to Indians. Oxen, on the other hand, actually improved on their hauling powers even after months of deprivation, and were content to munch coarse buffalo grass. They also conveniently provided a supply of 'jerked' (dried) meat if lameness or accidents required that they be butchered. Finally they were disdained by the Indians and were cheaper than horses.

One load which perhaps earned some adverse comment from friends and relatives was Samuel's library. They no doubt argued that so gross a weight was a fearful risk, for the experience of all emigrants was that loads grew heavier with every mile. The essential books worth carrying were a Bible, a dictionary, a hymn book and a grammar so that the children could continue their book-learning while actually trailing, surely a near perfect education. But for Samuel books appeared high on his list of priorities, and they were to remain with him night and day for many months until he saw them safely loaded on a Columbia River boat bound for Portland.

He calculated that the preliminary journey to Dudley would take four weeks. Before they left Caledonia they were joined by a neighbour Daniel Lucas, his wife and their three small sons. Lucas was a valuable acquisition, according to John Rogers, because he was experienced in frontier life, 'knowing all about camping and caring for the cattle', whereas Samuel and his family had never 'camped out a day in their lives'. Lucas brought two wagons and on their rear end-gates painted the single word 'Oregon'. On the first night they stayed with 'aunts, uncles and cousins' at Yorkville, and on the mext morning left to the accompaniment of a rousing send-off, as John Rogers describes in his autobiography: 'Looking back we saw the whole village of Yorkville walking along a little way, taking leave of aunts, uncles, cousins and acquaintances. We boys shook hands with the cousins and boys that were with us and then went scampering down the road.'

In the first week they trundled and sang through a familiar landscape of fall colours with night camps pitched at Vienna with its 'saw mill and a big frame hotel and the bedding fresh and clean', Delavan, Darien, Allen's Grove, Turtle Creek, where the night was cold and frosty and it was 'hard to keep warm', and then south of Beloit, 'a prosperous little place of neat cobblestone walled houses', across a 'broad prairie' into Illinois to make their Sunday rest at 'Mrs Moon's'. Her place was near the shallow and wide Rock River which made a lasting impression on John Rogers on account of 'the rapids falling over the limestone rocks, looking so clear, and the beautiful autumn leaves of the maple, butternut, walnut and hickory trees'.

The five wagons of the James and Lucas families were heading for the Mississippi. They passed through Kishuwaukie, noticing by the roadside small red flags fluttering on stakes driven into the ground which they understood marked a survey for a railroad to Chicago, and entered the town of Oregon, Illinois, no doubt pondering on how far they had to travel before they reached that other Oregon on the Willamette River. On a farm of rich prairie land they camped near a ruined log house that had been abandoned by some settler who had already decided to 'light out'[2] for the West. Here John Rogers remembered meeting a four-horse red mail coach, driven by a tall man wearing a stove-pipe hat who, looking like Abraham Lincoln (in retrospect of course), stared at the band of emigrants 'amused like'. Then they pushed on through Dixon, Como and

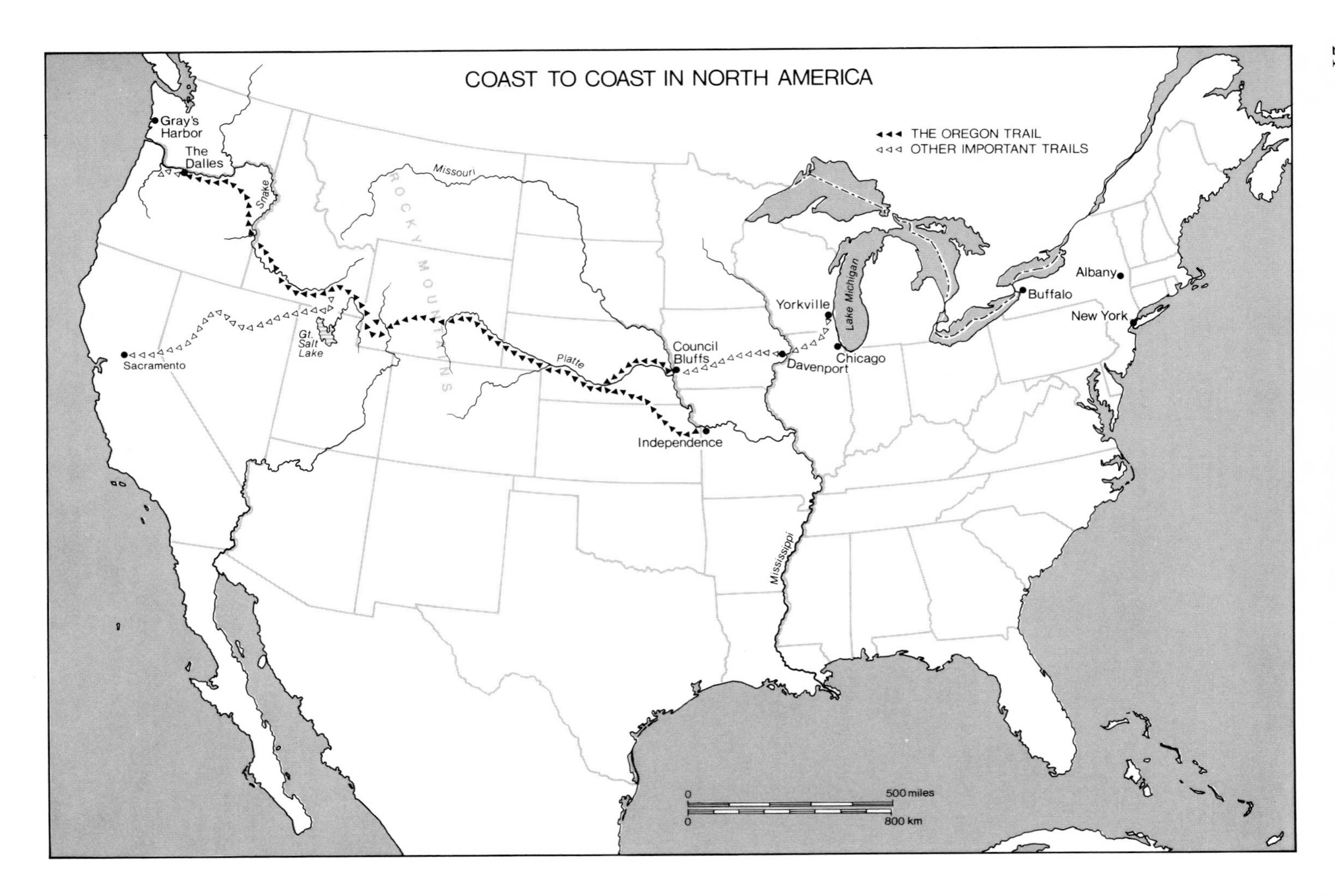
COAST TO COAST IN NORTH AMERICA
THE OREGON TRAIL
OTHER IMPORTANT TRAILS
Gray's Harbor
The Dalles
Snake
Missouri
ROCKY MOUNTAINS
Gt. Salt Lake
Sacramento
Platte
Council Bluffs
Independence
Davenport
Yorkville
Lake Michigan
Chicago
Mississippi
Buffalo
Albany
New York
0
500 miles
0
800 km

Prophet Town, crossed Rock River at Fair Port, marvelling the while at the cheap and abundant supplies of cheeses, hams and eggs until, by the end of the second week, they stood facing the Mississippi at Moline. Here they spent the sabbath of 20 October in prayer and worship 'at the Potters'.

Their third week began with assembling at Rock Island to take their place in the queue for the ferry, described by John Rogers as 'a boat with a tread power and two horses for engine power'. Once across the great river at Davenport, 'a snug little town on the Iowa side', they sensed that their great adventure was really about to begin. For one thing, they saw stretching before them the ceaseless prairie where 'it seemed as if all the settlers had to do was to build a cabin and break up the rich black prairie land and raise corn, pumpkins and fatten hogs and living comfortable.' For another, carelessness almost brought disaster down upon their innocent heads for 'fire came near burning up our wagons', as Samuel entered in his journal. However, they crossed the Cedar River without further incident and entered Iowa City, then a young settlement of no more than a hundred or so families but whose 'people had a busy industrious way about them', and whose children 'were well dressed and full of life', as John Rogers observed. It was here that Mrs James bought each of her two eldest boys a four-bladed pocket-knife, which they soon cherished as personal weapons to defend their lives and those of their parents 'when we should arrive in the Indian country'. However, there was the more immediate problem of crossing the city's river. It was their first experience of negotiating swiftly moving water without a ferry, fording on this occasion being achieved, says Samuel, 'with much danger'. By the end of the third week, they were camping 'at a blacksmith's', intentionally no doubt on account of repairs that needed to be done to the wagons after the fire. So Sunday 27 October resounded doubtless to the lusty and hearty singing of hymns and the musical chorus of hammers striking red-hot iron on anvils.

In the fourth week they picked up the trail again at Bear Creek, passed Marengo where 'a catamount [cougar] came near us in the night', forded Skunk River, and were somewhat unnerved by a 'bad hill'. On 1 November they rumbled through Newton and into a near-disaster. It had been continuously 'rainy', and Indian Creek was flooded. Luckily Lucas was at hand to sort out the trouble, 'a valuable man', comments John Rogers, for 'he had most of the characteristics of a Daniel Boone'. Though he could neither read nor write, he was 'consequently' very intelligent in practical matters. What happened was that just as it was getting dark the ox named Jack crowded its partner Dandy off the bridge, so that it was entangled in the harness and choking to death. Lucas swung his broad axe and with one 'lick' cut Dandy's hickory bow so that the animal fell to safety in the swollen river below. John Rogers was full of admiration for this demonstration by Lucas of his skill as a backwoodsman and pioneer. The hickory bow was two inches thick, yet Lucas cut through it with a single blow without even grazing the animal's neck.

After four more days and nights of heavy thunderstorms and torrential rain, the weary party plodded into Dudley. At first sight there seemed little to recommend the place. It was a one-street settlement just inside the fast growing state of Iowa, where in 1850 some two hundred thousand farmers and their families from the east were exploiting its deep and rich soil to produce almost nine million bushels of corn.[3] Its winters were bitterly cold and bleakly miserable, though perhaps not more so than in Wisconsin. It boasted no more than one hotel, one log cabin saloon and a general store which was also the post office. Its chief advantage was that it was in a forward position near Council Bluffs for an early start on the trail proper the following year, a fact which would not have escaped the circumspect Samuel. But there were other compensations to weigh. The truth was that in 1850 Dudley was a town of empty one-storey log cabins awaiting occupants, the dream-child of one Jeremiah Church, property developer and 'peripatetic builder'.

John Rogers describes Church as a 'dignified man who wore a stove-pipe hat and was distinguished as the only one in town who wore store clothes'. This was in contrast to the pioneers who wore homespun garments, usually of two colours, either a pale blue or a brownish butternut brindle and of so strong a weave that two suits were considered enough to last a lifetime, 'one for wedding and one for old age'. Church was waiting for tenants when the Cornish arrived, so Samuel had no problem in finding accommodation for his large family in a frame house next to the hotel. Lucas, however, regarded renting as the first step down the slippery slope to city life, so he simply went into a wood with his axe, felled some trees, and built his own log cabin a mile out of Dudley. However his cabin survived only a year like all the others in Dudley for the town soon disappeared. Church had unfortunately overlooked its geographical position in the south-west corner of Allen township in Polk county. The first cabins were erected near the Des Moines River about one mile south of the North River. A great storm burst the banks of the two rivers and drowned Dudley so that 'all its prospective importance went down the river to the Gulf'. Church, 'greatly disgusted', retired two miles to the interior and, not to be outdone by the forces of nature, started to build a new town he named Carlisle.[4]

But in 1850, when Samuel and his party arrived, Dudley was the centre of a very richly productive country whose corn harvest was of such a surprising abundance that it astonished him. In fact he was able to buy a field of standing corn, send his sons out to break off the ears, fill a wagon and haul it home to feed the oxen, recalls John Rogers. With the winter feed for the cattle assured, Samuel began to make full use of the short days and long nights for shaping his family through daily prayers, Bible readings and school lessons into the disciplined unit needed to master the mammoth tasks ahead. The two older boys Samuel and William melted bars of lead and ran the metal into moulds to make bullets and even baked bread, while their mother made or repaired their clothes, and their father no doubt wrestled with the problems of what provisions to buy.

Samuel does not give any details of these in his journal but, according to the guide books of the time, notably that written by Lansford Hastings, each and every emigrant needed 200 lbs of flour, 150 lbs of bacon, 20 lbs of coffee and sugar, and 10 lbs of salt, as well as some dried fruit, rice, beans, corn meal and peas. Whisky found its way on board for combating dysentery.[5] Samuel also had fashioned his own bowel-blasting pills.

Bacon, or 'sowbelly', was one of two main diets needed for survival (as well as being invaluable in an emergency for saving the lives of cattle that had drunk water poisoned by alkali salts). Dudley offered a plentiful supply of bacon flitches, the trade being in the hands of two brothers, Jack and Abe Shoemaker, who apparently employed John Rogers and his brother Tom to string up the flitches in the smoke-house. Samuel thus had immediate access to the best flitches for their mobile pantry! The other essential food was 'biscuit' or hard-tack, prepared by baking it in a Dutch oven and in large enough quantities to last most of the way to Oregon. On the plains, it is true, as long as the supply of flour lasted, it was possible to bake loaves of a fine brown consistency (especially in Wyoming where soda was plentiful and could be used as natural baking powder), but they were never eaten except as dessert with butter. The main filler throughout the journey was always to be the 'biscuit'. Samuel, ever inventive, designed a 'bread-worker', a trough to which he fixed a lever fashioned at one end like a brush. The dough was placed in the trough and it was the task of the boys to work the brush to and fro while the girls added the required measure of salt and water. It was necessary to knead the dough to the correct consistency and without the use of lard or butter so that the hard-tack would not become 'weevily'. When the kneading was finished, it was rolled out, cut into 'cracker shape' about four inches square, baked hard, and finally packed into 100 lb seamless grain sacks to keep company with similar sacks stuffed with sausages. All travellers soon grew tired of the sausage when it got strong, but hard-tack was always the main source of nourishment. It could be softened by dipping it in a cup of coffee, another item that no emigrant party could ever do without.

There were also important lessons to be learnt on the secret of becoming trail-wise, lessons that could only be demonstrated but never proved until the journey had started. Survival depended upon personal and family discipline which demanded immediate obedience. One way of ensuring this was for everyone to be given daily tasks, however repulsive their nature and however reluctant the receiver, for it was routine which guaranteed extra effort when spirits were flagging from loss of sleep, and always the grim prospect of yet another day of toil, aching backs and blistered hands under a glaring sun. John Rogers records that he and his brothers became skilled at making camp, building fires, frying meat, and cooking oat cakes by placing the dough in a pan until it became firm enough to stand by leaning it against a board in front of a fire. In the mornings they were expected to pack the bedding, clean and stow away all the cooking pots, and assist in rounding up and yoking the oxen. The boys soon discovered this was a complicated procedure. Two or three men would each take a yoke under his arm or over his right shoulder. After removing the bow from the yoke for the right (or off-side) ox, each would walk up to his assigned ox, slip the bow under the animal's neck and up through holes in the yoke and fasten it with a wooden bow key, which would then be turned flat-wise to prevent it from working itself out. Then the man would take out the other bow and stand back a little with the end of the yoke in the left hand and, motioning with the bow in the right hand, would call the next ox which docilely permitted the bow to be placed under its neck and fastened as before. When three yoke of oxen were ready, they were hitched to a wagon, one yoke at the tongue, one yoke in the swing and another in the lead. General usage describes two oxen as a yoke; two horses as a team; and two mules as a span.

The lead cattle were usually the best travellers and, as the Cornish discovered at Dudley, the most 'biddable' in the sense that they responded the most quickly to commands. The hindmost yoke on the tongue were called the 'wheelers', and were usually the heaviest cattle, being placed in that position because they could be relied upon in the most difficult terrain to serve as natural brakes when slithering down hills. This form of braking was usually assisted by the device of a chain lock or skid, fastened to the side of the wagon bed. But on exceptionally steep hills Samuel learned that a log chain could be fastened from the fore axle back to the rear wheel. On extreme downhill gradients, the chain was allowed to wrap itself round the rim and tyre, but this device, it was recommended, ought to be used as little as possible because of the strain on the wheel. Occasionally a stake, extending through the spokes of the rear wheels, served the same purpose.

One letter has survived from this winter at Dudley, written on 12 December 1850 by Samuel to his brother-in-law at Racine in Wisconsin, Thomas Foxwell.[6] In it he quotes another letter he had received from a Mr John, a one-time neighbour in Mullion, Cornwall, who was apparently highly critical of Samuel exchanging the 'abode of civilisation' in Wisconsin for the unknown in Oregon. Mr John elaborated that it would have been more sensible to emigrate to Australia where gold had been found, near Adelaide, 'in the sands of rivers in large quantities'.

Much of Samuel's letter, however, is concerned with health problems at Dudley, and his anxiety about his family's welfare. He reported to his brother-in-law that he, his 12-year old son William, and his Wisconsin friend Lucas had all been very ill of a disorder which he diagnosed as influenza. They all suffered so 'immensely' from pains in the head that he thought they could 'hardly survive'. Some of their neighbours did not: 'One strong young man of about 21 or 22 years of age was taken ill before us a few days and he did not live over 8 or 10 days, and a young married woman of about the same age, remarkably stout and healthy, was seized in a somewhat similar manner except that her stomach was the part principally affected and she did not live over 4 or 5 days.'

But the ever resourceful Samuel 'trusted to the use of my own pills'. So they all survived, but were humble enough to be 'exceedingly grateful to our Heavenly Father for his sparing mercies towards us'.

NOTES

1. Merrill J. Mattes, *The Great Platte River Road* (Nebraska State Historical Society, Publications 25, 1969), p. 16.
2. 'To light out' is the vernacular phrase used by Mark Twain to describe Huckleberry Finn's decision to wander westwards to avoid being 'civilized' again.
3. Ray Billington, *Westward Expansion*, p. 478.
4. J. M. Dixon, *A Centennial History of Polk County, Iowa* (1876), pp. 54, 55.
5. Mattes, p. 46.
6. This letter is in the possession of the Foxwells of Elgin, Iowa, to whom the authors are grateful for their permission to quote.

CHAPTER 4

Final Preparations at Council Bluffs

On 8 April with 'spring coming on', says John Rogers, 'we hitched up the faithful oxen and started out for Council Bluffs.' They rode out of Dudley on crests of unbounded optimism and cheerfulness across a vast prairie of black loam interspersed with groves of timber and newly settled homes surrounded by tracts of vacant land. But all too soon they experienced an unexpected set-back. By the end of the first week the fourteen-year-old William was 'very sick of lung fever', a type of pneumonia not uncommon in families that lived too close to rivers, as at Dudley. He ran so high a temperature and fever that Samuel was compelled to stop and camp for three days at Winterset until the boy's strength returned due to the providential appearance on the trail of an English doctor. So it was not until 21 April that the Cornish party arrived in Council Bluffs (or rather Kanesville, as it was then known) after an anxious drive of 145 miles, according to the odometer or viameter that Samuel had fixed on one of the wagon wheels, an idea he had borrowed from the Mormons. Indeed he had led his family into Mormon territory.

The name Council Bluffs was older than that of Kanesville and had been given by the explorers Lewis and Clark in 1804 to the place where they had parleyed with Indians. The significance of that historic occasion, however, seems to have been forgotten when the Mormons built their winter quarters there in preparation for their own conquest of the road to their promised land. These quarters were evacuated in 1847 when the pioneer party set out for Utah; it embraced 148 persons, 72 wagons, 43 horses, 52 mules, 66 oxen, 19 cows, 17 dogs and an unstated number of chickens. A small detachment of Mormons was left behind and it was they who called their settlement Kanesville in honour of their gentile friend, one Thomas Leper Kane.[1] The Mormons intended it to be a permanent emigration station, though this rear party only survived the first winter by digging out caves in the hill-sides where some of them were still living when the Cornish arrived. Kanesville was splendidly situated, for it marked the starting point of the most important of all the highroads to the west, that imposing natural highway later known as the Platte River Road, but in Samuel's time referred to as the Council Bluffs Road. Once on this road, the emigrant would find himself stepping out to the Sweetwater River, then to South Pass and the Continental Divide and so the point of no return. Kanesville in 1850 was becoming the major assembly point for crossing the wide Missouri because all Mormons in their highly organised 'companies' from the east and from Europe passed through it to join what was rapidly becoming known as the Mormon Trail, which Samuel was now to follow.

A well-informed man, it is more than likely that he read the Kanesville *Frontier Guardian*, whose editor had written enthusiastically from time to time about the many advantages of Kanesville over that other assembly point, Independence, Missouri. Cholera seemed to strike there less frequently.[2] The Mormon Trail was the shorter, for Kanesville was 200 miles nearer to Fort Laramie than Independence, and it was also the easiest to negotiate. Though timber was scarce and the trail in parts ridged with dangerous buffalo tracks over which wagon-wheels bumped and animals stumbled, the Platte River Road was dry, reasonably level with a fair abundance of grass, and was as broad as any turnpike in England, as a traveller in 1850 declared.[3] Consequently, argued Samuel, the Mormon Trail meant a considerable saving of time, energy, money, cattle and stores.

The Mormon influence in Kanesville, however, seems to have been too strong for Mrs James. In this settlement of some three hundred and fifty log cabins by a small stream in a deep hollow,[4] only a few miles from the Missouri, described by John Rogers as a 'wide valley between high hills' or bluffs, a large Mormon train was assembling bound for Utah. It consisted almost entirely of emigrants from England under the captaincy of an English 'bishop'. Samuel thought he and his wife ought to make him a social call but the visit almost ended in disaster for, as John Rogers reports: 'Mother gave him a piece of her mind. The idea of an Englishman becoming so depraved and misleading those poor ignorant proselytes aroused all of her British ire.' No doubt Samuel gently urged her to calm down by reminding her that their future safety depended almost entirely on Mormon advice and experience for, next to trappers and mountain men, they were the most reliable cartographers of the trails, if not all of the way to Oregon, at least to Green River and the Snake River. In his rough and ready journal he records that it was in Kanesville that he bought a Mormon guide-book and that the names of the places he mentions in his journal were all of Mormon origin.

There were several guide-books to be bought in Kanesville, for instance those by E. Sanford Seymore and Joseph E. Ware, Lansford Hastings and Joel Palmer,[5] as well as the columns of the local *Guardian* with its oft-repeated advice on the need to 'treat the Indians with kindness as long as you can, but never suffer them to come within the circle of your encampment'.[6] Another book that Samuel most likely carried with him was the famous Mormon publication written by William Clayton in 1848 and widely distributed in the eastern states.[7]

Though useful only as far as the Great Salt Lake it was authoritative because Clayton was the official historian of the 1847 pioneers. Born in Lancashire, England, he emigrated in 1841 to join the Mormon Church, became secretary to Brigham Young, and was a member of the pioneer party that opened up the main trail to Utah along the North Platte River. His guide-book at five dollars was a rich source of information for the would-be emigrant with its detail of the geography of the trail, the distances from one place of rest to another, where and where not to camp, in short how to keep alive. Perhaps too Samuel sensed some spiritual link with Clayton for they were both refugees from the 'Hungry Forties' economic depression in England.

Camping close to the Missouri under some large cottonwood trees, Samuel's stay near Kanesville was short, no more than a week. It was time to go when about 40 families and their wagons had assembled and organised themselves into a meeting to elect a Mr McCartney as captain of the train. Young Samuel James and 'Gus', Lucas's hired man, then took a can of coal tar and painted a number, one, two, three and so on up to 26, on the covers of each wagon. On the first day they were to move off in that strict numerical order; on the second day No. 2 wagon would take the place of No. 1 which would then go to the rear; on the third day No. 3 would be in the lead, while No.2 would take the rear; and so on until all had taken their turn as lead. The idea behind this democratic arrangement was to ensure that each wagon, the draught animals, the teamsters and the emigrants would all have an equal chance of avoiding the clouds of dust billowing from the 25 wagons in front for at least one day in 26.

Samuel knew that dust was a major problem. A cloud could be so thick and impenetrable that a driver could not even see his lead oxen. If combined with a head wind, and the winds usually blew from the west, the dust flew into the eyes like needles, setting up the most painful irritation. But much of the trouble could be avoided by using dark glasses, and Samuel records that he bought several pairs for the use of his family and teamsters. They could be useful in another way. The teamsters usually walked on the near or left side of a wagon but often, to avoid the choking dust, they would move over to the right and then confuse the oxen which had been trained to walk with their drivers on the left. By using goggles they did not need to change positions. Of course the teamsters were not alone in walking the trail. Most of the emigrants foot-slogged every one of those 2,000 miles to Oregon step by step, day after day, their feet bruised, swollen, cracked and forever aching, often without water to soothe them.

And so the last purchases and final preparations were made as the deadline for departure drew near. Samuel checked his inventory of cooking vessels, water keg, tin canisters to hold milk, a small grindstone on which to sharpen his butcher knives, lead bullets, rifle and shotgun, strong spare shoes and boots, clothes to last a year and no more, spare ox shoes, hammers, nails, saws, as well as bedding and blankets, food in sacks, and cotton shirts, tobacco, fish hooks, bells and mirrors for trading with the Indians—and all to be stowed away and their whereabouts known so that they were rapidly accessible at a moment's notice. Everyone was now so engaged in last minute adjustments to their plans that the town must have been a hive of activity and excitement. Men, women and children from almost every country in Europe and from every state east of the Mississippi seemed crowded in this babel of a Babylon that had a pentecostal ring about it. John Rogers captures the heady atmosphere and thrill of anticipation now that the adventure was really about to begin: 'The Yankee drawl and nasal twang, the southern accent of the negro, the high pitch of the Cornishman, the burr of the north-country Englishman and his cousin the Scot, the throaty roll of the Welshman, the rich brogue of the quick-witted Irishman, the guttural Dutchman and the musical Spaniard were heard on every side.' As for himself it was now that he 'began to get a scent of the great plains' as he made his final climb of the hills to gaze 'away off over the boundless plains to the West, the wide bow of the Missouri and the occasional smoke of a steamboat'.

On the eve of the crossing, a Sunday and a rest day for the Cornish, Samuel sat down to his last task, that of writing a farewell letter to his brother-in-law, Thomas Foxwell, dated 27 April 1851. The address is 'Banks of the Missouri, 3 miles from Kanesville, Pottawottomie County, Iowa'.[8] He describes the party as consisting of himself, Anna Maria, their eight children and three drivers 'who drive for their board'. They were Alanson Pomeroy from Illinois, Benjamin Franklin from New York State, and Alexander McCloy from Ohio. All of them were reputed to be 'choice hands about 20 to 22 or 23 years of age and well educated and behaved'. Samuel emphasised that Pomeroy was likely to be their most valuable guarantor of success for he 'has been through before'. Indeed, Samuel explained, at the age of twelve he had accompanied his parents in the party that Lansford Hastings and Dr Elijah White had led to Oregon in 1842, and in 1846 had made the return journey as a teenager with Captain Palmer and sixteen others, 'packing on horses and mules, being about 50 to the 18 men', and meeting up with Judge Thornton's party near Fort Laramie. J. Quinton Thornton and his party were taking advantage of the 1846 acquisition of Oregon Territory by compromise, though in that year emigration was light on account of the fate of the Donner party in the snows of the Sierra Nevada, due to the unreliable information in Lansford Hastings's guide book.

Pomeroy proved to be a hive of information, experience and reassurance for Samuel, who was worried whether their health would suffer on the trail. Not at all, said Pomeroy. 'When Pomeroy was returning to Independence with Palmer', wrote Samuel, 'they had no tent to lie under and merely threw their blankets or buffalo robes on the ground and lay down, sometimes thoroughly drenched with rain before morning, yet every one enjoyed the best of health all the way and when they arrived at St Joseph in Missouri felt quite oppressed in entering the houses, being accustomed for a long time to the open air.' And as for the climate of Oregon, Pomeroy confirmed all that Samuel had read. The winters were so mild that 'running water never freezes south of the Columbia and the ponds seldom and when they do generally not thicker than window glass.' One winter had been so mild that Pomeroy had eaten strawberries on the last day of January. Neither were the summers excessively hot. The 'face' of the country in Oregon was 'beautifully diversified', with 'hill, valley, streamlet and mountain and groves and prairies, abundance of small hills on which timber usually grows, while the prairies are seldom larger than a mile or two wide, and 3 or 4 miles long.' The settlers lived 'abundantly easier' than elsewhere on the continent, and so did the cattle. He had never seen a 'clip of hay' because grass was so plentiful which 'starts a-growing early in October like Spring and keeps green and growing all winter'.

So, concluded Samuel, he and his family were ready for their stirring adventure. They were well equipped for their stock consisted of three wagons, 11 yoke of oxen and two yoke of cows, one yoke of oxen being owned by driver McCloy and half of another yoke by Chapman. Tomorrow they would be across the Missouri, 'the extreme boundary of anything like civilised life', where 'you are among the savages and the wilderness, a fruitful topic for explanation.' Yet, he hastened to add, 'our strength is on high and I feel happy in the protection of the Almighty.'

From where he sat Samuel described the landscape around him, 'true English scenery' of 'sharp hills and narrow valleys and glens, the hills perfectly rich and fruitful to the top'. The banks of the Missouri, he thought, resembled some parts of the coasts of England, high broken sandy bluffs with a little timber and short grass similar to 'the Cury and Gunwalloe towans' in Cornwall (towans being dunes of blown sand). Between the bluffs was the bottom land, very rich and level and about five or six miles wide, through which wound the Missouri, 'a perfect puddle of fine sand and dirt'. He had sampled its water and concluded that 'foul as it is, it tastes better than some we have had even from wells' and considered that it was even more 'healthful' on account of its being 'quite cold'. The prospect of reaching Oregon City, still some 1,800 miles away, before the end of September, did not unduly daunt him now: 'It does not appear such an awful journey to me now as it did once. I have already travelled 900 miles since leaving Racine . . . and besides it will be summer.' They would be travelling in a caravan of 30 wagons for safety's sake, but 'once past the Pawnees' they intended to divide into small companies 'for convenience'.

Finally, expressing his sorrow over the death of 'Aunt Trigg' who, he trusted, was now gathered safely 'into the Heavenly Garner as a shock of corn fully ripe for the sickle', he said his farewell, 'though we trust not a last one', and left space for his wife Anna Maria to pen a message to her mother and friends. More anxious and fearful than her husband, she writes as if she sensed that there could never be a reunion with them and clings to her memories of happier and less troubled days:

> I must now bid you adieu. My heart feels as though it would break and yet I feel more support than I ever expected to feel. I have seen different ones here, between sixty and seventy years and I wish you were among them and yet I think all is for the best and cannot feel thankful enough for having been brought [here] . . . Tell Susan I did not receive the lock of your hair but have not forgotten golden ringlets that once waved on your brow nor the white locks that last met my eye in Yorkville. O may we meet where pain and parting will be no more. Farewell my dearest friends.

The letter left Council Bluffs on 3 May. By then Anna Maria and Samuel were approaching Pawnee country, no doubt apprehensive of what courage they could muster to resist their threats.

NOTES

1. Merrill J. Mattes, *The Great Platte River Road*, pp. 122, 123.
2. John D. Unruh Jr., *The Plains Across* (University of Illinois, 1975), pp. 68, 72, 73.
3. Mattes, p. 10.
4. Ibid., p. 124.
5. E. Sanford Seymore, *Emigrants' Guide to the Gold Mines of Upper California* (Chicago, R. L. Wilson, Daily Journal Office, 1849), 104 pp.; Joseph E. Ware, *The Emigrants' Guide to California* (first published in 1848, it was republished in 1932 by Princeton University Press), 63 pp.; Lansford Hastings, *The Emigrants' Guide to Oregon and California*, 1845 (reproduced in facsimile in 1932 from the 1845 edition by Princeton University Press), 159 pp.; and Joel Palmer, *Journal of Travels over the Rocky Mountains to the Mouth of the Columbia River, made during the years 1845 and 1846* (Cincinnati, J. A. and U. P. James, 1847), 189 pp. Palmer's book was perhaps by far the best of the four. Not only were directions given explicitly and simply, but Palmer had made two very successful trips all the way to Oregon's Pacific coast. Seymore and Ware were more useful for emigrants to California and of no use at all beyond Fort Hall, near Boise, for Oregon travellers. Hastings was suspect because he had recommended a route to California which he had never seen, leading to the notorious tragedy of the Donner party: see Gregory M. Franza, *The Oregon Trail Revisited* (Patrice Press, St Louis, Missouri,1972, p. 23).
6. Unruh, p. 75.
7. William Clayton, *The Latter-Day Saints' Emigrants' Guide* (St Louis, Chamber and Knapp, 1848), 24 pp.
8. This letter also is in the possession of the Foxwells of Elgin, Iowa, whom the authors thank for permission to quote.

CHAPTER 5

To Fort Laramie

On a Monday morning, 28 April 1851, Samuel and his family took up their positions in the long queue of wagons and cattle waiting to cross the swift, turbulent and muddy Missouri on the Mormon ferry. This was a flat boat, propelled by six rowers and capable of carrying two wagons at a time. John Rogers sat in the first of the three Cornish wagons and, as he landed on the Nebraska side, stole a quick sympathetic backward glance at his mother in the driver's seat of the second wagon: 'As she looked out over the border of the great plains we were about to embark upon, the tears were coming to her eyes which kind of made me sober.'

And so the long anticipated adventure was now really happening as they rounded up the stock that had swum the river and no doubt marvelled at the grassy plain that unrolled itself before them. The soil looked good, but the landscape mysteriously empty and unoccupied, for the only timber was restricted to fringes of cottonwood along the streams. At first progress was slow, no more than 20 miles in five days. It included a forced camp of three days so that Lucas could brand their cattle with his DL sign on their horns, passage through another Mormon winter quarters of caves dug into the bluffs, and an early brush with Pawnee Indians. Shouting and gesticulating, they rode alongside the wagons in double file on their bare-back ponies, using lariats of hair as halters and bridles. Samuel had read that usually they were only well-meaning scroungers who demanded payment for passage through their lands.[1] They appeared harmless enough but one of the teamsters warned Samuel that they probably concealed weapons beneath their buffalo robes. On hearing this, he paid up, not anticipating that worse would follow three days later.

Before them flowed the Elkhorn River, the first of the Platte River tributaries. It was only about three feet deep, but deceptive on account of its swift current. Here again ferrying was the monopoly of the Mormons who charged a dollar a wagon. But once across, they were again troubled by the Indians who this time demanded not money, but more valuable tribute, as Samuel ruefully recorded on 5 May: 'Small lakes, difficulties with the Pawnees, let them have two cows and some flour'. On the next day, further payments were exacted: 'Shell Creek, second difficulty with Pawnees, let them have one cow and some flour'. And John Rogers remembered with horror that, as soon as the deal was made, the Indians immediately slaughtered the cow for food and cut it up in pieces before their very eyes. These were serious losses for Samuel and nothing short of tragedies for the children, for they nursed a close affection for all animals and especially for the milch cows. All resourceful pioneers took along milch cows to keep the family healthy for usually they could be relied upon to provide enough milk until they reached the frightening alkali deserts of Wyoming. Samuel started with five whose names are some indication of the affection lavished upon them by these Cornish children—Spotty, Linsey, Sukey, Nutsey, and old Spaney, a strong long-horned Texan which they loved to ride, though a hard and difficult milker. Samuel eventually parted with her and the protests of the children can well be imagined, as well as those of their mother, for to her fell the responsibility of milking and butter-making, both now reduced in supply. She milked the cows in the early morning light, and strained the milk into a wooden churn, which she then fixed to the back of a wagon. By the end of the day its constant jolting produced a small ball of butter and even perhaps a small amount of milk sweet enough to quench their thirst. Usually the evening's yield of milk was consumed with the main meal.

The Indians came a third time, planting themselves between where the pioneers intended to camp and a spring of water. The men hurriedly formed a circle for the protection of the women and children, and prepared for an attack. The fact that none came was due to the bravery of Alanson Pomeroy. Nonchalantly he picked up a couple of buckets and marched through the band of Indians to the spring, returning to his wagon without even spilling a drop of water. Both Indians and whites were impressed and the tension eased.

Progress so far was slow, only 66 miles in nine days, and in the next week was no faster. On 8 May they arrived at a fork of the Loup River, the next tributary of the Platte. The evening was stormy and, as if that was not enough to try their tempers after a hard day's walking, they found themselves in the middle of a skirmish between Pawnees and Sioux. This was not unusual at this time of the year for they rarely fought in the winter, and only emerged in the spring to stake out their claims to disputed territory. Unfortunately, of course, their appearance coincided with that of the emigrants. So the cattle were hurriedly driven across the river 'in the yoke', while Samuel assisted in pushing wagons 'by hand' on to the Mormon ferry-boat, fortunately without loss because the soft soil of its banks and quicksands made the Loup a tricky stream.[2]

Once across, Samuel was highly delighted to find already encamped a large train of wagons bound for California, whose gold hunters had halted to await likely reinforcements in case the Pawnees and Sioux decided to smoke their pipe of peace and attack them. So, for mutual protection and because of continuous

Left Beardsly Vale Oct 5th 1850
Oct. 6 - Yorkville - Sunday.
7 Vienna. First out camp
8 Delavan passing through Darien a good country
9 Allen's Grove. very rainy
10 Hill near Turtle Creek. Very cold frosty night
11 Crossed a broad prairie in Illinois South of Beloit
12 Mr. Moore's
13 Sunday. No travel
14 Farm Place. Passed Kishwaukie, beautiful view
15 Near Rock River. Passed by Oregon City
16 Old Log House. Passed through Dixon
17 Farm House. Passed by Como & through Prophets Town
18 Fair Port ferry on Rock river
19 Mr. Brook's. Crossed Rock river at Fairport ferry & came to the Mississippi. Passed through Moline.
20 Sunday. No travel.
21 At the Potter's. Crossed the Mississippi from Rock Island to Davenport.
22 On the Prairie. Fire came near burning up our waggons.
23 Cedar River Ferry. Passed through Tipton
24 Allen's Grove in Iowa
25 Iowa City Mills. Passed through Iowa City Forded Iowa river, with much danger.
26 At a Blacksmith's
27 Sunday. No travel
28 Bear Creek. Passed by Marengo. A catamount came near us in the night
29 Talbot's
30 Latimer's Grove
31 Henshaw's Crossed the Skunk river Bad Hill
Nov 1 Branch of Indian Creek. Passed through Newton very rainy. Waggon upset in the creek, going over a bad bridge.
2 Another branch of Indian Creek
3 Sunday - No travel
4 Prairie Near Mitchell's. Heavy thunder-storm in the night.
5 Dudley - About in all 400 miles

Left Dudley April 8th 1851 — miles

		miles
Apr. 8	Camped at Pearson's	10
9	Farm	15
10	Farm	15
11	Prairie, passed through Winterset	18
12	Prairie, passed through Wah-ta-wah	16
13	Sunday, Prairie on lower 3 river	16
14	Hedgl's on the Nodoway river	8
15	Nishnabotony & Indian Town	20
16, 17, 18	In Camp William very sick of Lung fever.	
19	Oman's	15
20	Sunday. Silver Trout	12
21	Kanesville	18
		163

Very bad miry roads all the way nearly

Crossed the Missouri River — miles

		miles
April 28	& camped on Prairie	18
29, 30, May 1st	Lay in camp	
May 2	Camped at a Slough passed through Mormon Winter Quarters	
3	Pappea	8
4	Sunday. Elkhorn ferried at one dollar a waggon	9
5	Small Lakes. Difficulty with the Pawnees, let them have 2 Cows & some flour	16
6	Shell Creek second difficulty with Pawnees they had 1 Cow & some flour	19¾
7	Lake South of the road	13¼
8	Loup Fork Ferry very stormy night Battle of the Pawnees & Sioux. Drove the cattle across in the yoke & pushed the waggons into the boat by hand	5
9	Lay in Camp. Stormy	
10	Prairie Little grass	12
11	Sunday. Prairie better grass. 15 Waggons left us so that from 36 we were reduced to 21 waggons	2
12	Prairie	20
13	Plain, no wood, Antelopes. Alarm of Indians at night. Grass good	20
14	Wood River violent thunder Storm	28
15	Platte. Bridged Wood River	5
16	Prairie good grass, no wood or water under a mile	20
17	Elm Creek, poor grass. Bad management & over driving	29
18	Sunday. Platte by some Islands. Great deal of cold rain. Every thing wet	15
19	Willow Lake, feed not very good. Bad management hurrying off the cattle in the mornings before they have well fed.	20
20	Prairie near Platte river	23
21	By a Spring, Dreadful Hail Storm. Advised to lie down in my wet clothes to prevent catching cold, tried the experiment but don't want to try it again, caught a coldness if not a cold that very nearly used me up. Some waggon tongues & wheels broken by the unruly cattle during the storm.	23
22	Last Timber Cold & misty. ~~Horses~~ failing fast. Cannot be trusted to feed so easily as cattle, nor can they feed so fast, besides the bad weather hurts them more. First Buffalo seen to day 302¼ miles from Winter Quarters	12
23	North Bluff Fork weather clear fine and peculiarly elastic — First Stampede of the cattle.	16
24	Picannini Creek	23
25	Two Miles West of Camp Creek	23
26	Sand Hill Creek	22

One of my waggons crossing the quick sands of Castle creek stuck fast, took out, carried over

Margin notes: Omahas; Pawnees; united with California train for protection; Shians storms of wind and rain, they all decided not to move for another 24 hours. Violent storms in the Platte valley were a frequent occurrence in May and burst with unpredictable swiftness and severity. A day would begin with oppressive heat, arousing murmuring clouds of gnats and mosquitoes, followed at noon by a darkening of the sky, the noise of a howling wind and then blasts of hail and sleet which Francis Parkman in his *The Oregon Trail* (1846) likened to a 'storm of needles', which were met full on the face because the wind blew directly from the west. Days of drizzling rain followed, the choking dust was transformed into lakes of mud and in three days Samuel's wagons advanced only five miles. 'Lay in camp, stormy weather', he tersely commented.

These were difficult and tiresome days, some worse than others. Wood River was usually easily crossed, being but 12 feet wide and one foot deep, but not so on this occasion in the teeth of a violent thunderstorm and torrential rain which made the animals frenzied with fright. There also seems to have been some disagreement among the teamsters, for on 11 May fifteen wagons of the original train from Kanesville went their own way, leaving Samuel's train reduced to twenty-one. He was now complaining almost daily about the lack of timber for firing to dry their clothes and equipment, but more often about the teamsters exhausting the horses and oxen. On 17 May, after a drive of 29 miles, he wrote: 'Elm Creek, poor grass, bad management and over-driving'. The next day proved equally miserable and demoralising: 'Sunday. River Platte by some islands, great deal of cold rain, everything wet'. Monday saw no improvement: 'Willow Lake, feed not very good, bad management, hurrying of cattle in the morning before they have well fed'.

They were now well within the valley of the Platte and noticing, with some alarm, its unusual flatness and dreary monotony, though John Rogers later recalled that the 'bold cliffs to our right were a great attraction to us boys'. These were scorched and desolate bluffs formed by wind-blown sand which produced a curious optical illusion. As the sun played on the shimmering water of the river, between one and two miles wide, with its low banks of loose sand and its dearth of trees, apart from an occasional willow, poplar or cottonwood, it took on the appearance of a sea with the sand dunes as its coastline. Indeed Platte really means flat water and is synonymous with the Omaha Indian word for Nebraska. R. L. Stevenson found its flatness almost hypnotic, describing it in his *Across the Plains* as 'a world almost without feature; an empty sky; and empty earth; the great plain ran until it touched the skirts of heaven—no landmark but that unattainable evening sun for which they steered and which daily fled them'.

Opposite: *Two pages from Samuel James's Diary, October–November 1850 and April–May 1851. The figures on the right-hand side show the daily mileage.* Photograph, slightly reduced in size, by courtesy of David James

The Platte River. Photograph Helen Arbuckle, San José, California

The Platte River was a problem to the unwary traveller. Though only a few inches deep, its water could be deceptively swift with a moving sandy bottom that made it too dirty even for washing, still less for drinking. Francis Parkman tasted the Platte water only once and complained that the sand grated on his teeth, setting them on edge. Others desisted after contracting diarrhea. So, too shallow to be ferried over and too wide to be bridged, the only possible way across was to ford it and that was a terrifying hazard because it was pitted with sandbars, quicksands and occasional deep water[3] which could swallow a wagon and its contents in no time at all.

Then there was yet another ever-present danger. The Platte was the natural waterhole for herds of buffalo. Hundreds of them pounded the earth on their way to and from the river, crossing and recrossing their tracks as they felt inclined, the thunder of their hooves and the clouds of dust sending Samuel's cattle wild with apprehension and fright. With eyes glazed, the oxen, he tells us, would raise their heads and make frantic efforts to break loose from their harness. The buffalo tracks became deep grooves running at right angles to the emigrant trail, producing a ridge road over which the wagons bounced and lurched, adding to the oxen's confusion. Colliding with a thousand pound beast had to be avoided at all costs, but this concentrated mass of muscle and hide paradoxically provided the emigrants with an unexpected but essential commodity, the buffalo 'chip' (dung). Where there was little dry grass and no sage for fuel, it was one of the blessings of bountiful nature that the ungainly buffalo provided an excellent substitute. Its droppings, light to handle and dry as a bone after years of exposure on the sun-baked plains, burned almost like charcoal, made no blaze and little smoke, and threw out a fierce aromatic heat. As they walked alongside the wagons John Rogers and his brothers had the daily task of gathering them in bags to ensure the evening fire for washing and the baking of bread. The usual procedure for this was for their mother to make up the dough at mid-day, the period of rest known as 'nooning', though this could be at any convenient time. In the evening, before going to bed, she dug a hole in or near the camp fire, placed the dough in a baking kettle with a heavy lid on top, and then deposited it in the hole under a covering of some red hot chips and plenty of ashes. In the morning she raked out the ashes, opened the kettle and produced a loaf of fine brown bread. This was a luxury to be eaten as dessert with butter, for the normal fare was still the hard-tack.

By now, the third week in May, Samuel was having more trouble with the oxen. Not only had they been overworked by the teamsters in their hurry to reach Fort Laramie, but they were suffering and getting weaker on account of the continual storms, as he was. On 21 May he recorded being forced to halt near a spring because of a 'dreadful hail storm' with unpleasant and dangerous consequences: 'advised to lie down in my wet clothes to prevent catching cold, tried the experiment, but don't want to try it again, caught a cold that very nearly used me up'. In the midst of these miseries, his 'unruly' draught animals, equally miserable and frantic with no shelter against the aerial bombardment, tugged and strained at the harness, snapped the tongue or pole in two and broke one of the wheels. How Samuel handled this calamity we do not know. Tongue, spokes and axles were very easily broken and spare parts were usually carried. Broken spokes could be removed and new ones inserted. Even wagon rims could be repaired by resetting them when the wheel had been soaked in water and wedging them with buffalo hide.[4] But a broken wheel was a much more serious matter. Perhaps Samuel, with his usual foresight, did carry a spare; if not, then he would have had to find an abandoned wheel. He was discovering that his working horses were 'failing fast'. They were quite unable to face the shocking weather 'for the bad weather hurts them more' than the oxen, they would not forage the dry grass of the plains, they were easily plagued by insects, and they often contracted distemper through drinking the tepid water of the Platte.[5] By now they were more of a liability than an asset and so were expendable.

It was on 22 May, '302$\frac{1}{4}$ miles from winter quarters' at Kanesville, that the Jameses saw their first buffalo. On 23 May, as they forded North Bluff fork, the skies miraculously cleared and the weather turned 'fine and peculiarly elastic' Samuel reported, though with an unexpected effect on the cattle for without warning they stampeded. Apparently this was not unusual near the forks of the Platte, what with the occasional lightning flash, the constant downpouring of the rain and the shouting of the teamsters who wanted to reach Fort Laramie as quickly as possible. But, after this excitement, rain and hail were to be cooling memories, for the James family now faced weeks of tedious walking under blistering suns over the hot prairie, the air swarming with sand flies and mosquitos as the North Platte did its best to survive, leaving treacherous quicksands to trap the careless. On 24 May at Sand Hill Creek Samuel was caught off guard, although the guide book had warned him of 'low banks, but not good to cross on account of quicksands'. One of his wagons stuck fast in a quicksand near Castle Creek and 'was sinking, sinking all the time,' he wrote. Quickly he lightened the load by pulling out his wife and children, threw them on a sand-bar in the middle of the creek, and 'got the wagon started' again. Rapid action was essential for the wagon had to be kept moving at all costs.

Young John Rogers witnessed a different incident, an Indian killing a buffalo with bow and arrows, not an easy target unless you knew exactly its area of vulnerability. On a fast pony he 'cut' or separated his quarry from the herd that was drinking in the shallow part of the river, discharging arrow after arrow into its side close to the foreleg about one-third of the way up the body. Six arrows were enough to bring the heavy and clumsy beast to the ground, whereupon the Indian dragged the carcass to the shore, skinned it, dismembered it, ate the entrails, and then rode into camp to offer a large chunk of fresh meat to Samuel, no doubt as a starter for trading or to reconnoitre the strength of the emigrants. Samuel, it appears, bought from them two ponies for his boys to be used for driving the loose stock along the trail, but he seems to have been a worried man. On 27 May, there occurred a second stampede in which he lost his best ox. It was so valuable and treasured by the children that he sent out his hunters to search for it. Then on 29 May there were more 'desertions' from the main train so that it was now reduced to ten wagons, hardly enough to counter an Indian attack. However, all the indications so far showed that the Indians were not hostile, at least as far as Fort Laramie. The trail here was littered with buffalo skulls, weathered to so smooth and white a finish that they were used as writing pads to warn or encourage on-coming emigrants. One message John Rogers picked up from the desert floor was dated 23 June and read: 'Party of Sioux came into camp, friendly, gave us quite a lot of fresh buffalo meat'.

Reduced numbers probably account for Samuel's taking advantage of the chance to hire an extra hand. A teamster brought into camp—from where we know not—a 'cousin'. The Cornish are not likely to have enquired into the exact relationship, the phrase being common in their own vocabulary, but he was a tough and formidable figure to the children, as he towered above them with his long hair and buckskin jacket. Perhaps he had been trapping with the mountain men along the rivers and mountains of the west, for he claimed that he had been a companion of Kit Carson and J. C. Fremont on their 'exploring trips'. His name was William Carson Stone.

On 30 May the travellers were all excited to see, some 30 miles away on the western horizon, the outline of a landmark they had been eagerly anticipating in country that Samuel could only describe as 'most romantic and strange looking'. It was the spectacular Chimney Rock,[6] a column of limestone and sandstone, no more than a few feet in diameter but about 300 feet high, and the lower part 'a conical mound rising out of the naked plain', as Captain Benjamin Bonneville described it when he first saw it in 1832.[7] When John Rogers picked it out in the clear desert air he thought it seemed no larger than a tree trunk and it continued to fascinate him from the time when it came into view until the time when it vanished on the eastern horizon. 'I never got tired looking at it', he observed. It was the companion of all these weary travellers for as much as four days for, moving at the rate of 12 or so miles a day, they saw it two days before they reached it and two days after leaving it. But Chimney Rock was also more than a landmark. It was a time-mark that clocked their progress and renewed their hopes in a future just at the time when their spirits were flagging. Standing alone in the middle of a gap between two immense bluffs, this most unusual monument of the entire trail signalled a welcome to a tomorrow's oasis of rich green meadows. But in Samuel's time, this was hardly a place in which to linger, for it was near Chimney Rock that in the two previous years the scourge of Asiatic cholera had struck hard at emigrants weakened by privation. Carried by rats on ships sailing between Asiatic ports and New Orleans, then on vessels up the Mississippi and so to the points of embarkation west, in 1849 cholera accounted for almost two thousand emigrants perishing on the trail and in 1850 more than a thousand.[8] John Rogers perhaps was unaware of these calamities and was more interested and excited by what he saw beyond the pillared rock, the summit of Laramie Peak, lonely and remote and snow-covered, a hard day's riding away.

On the last day of May and after another 20 miles of snorting and panting oxen struggling with the wagons between mounds and bluffs among badlands in searing heat and choking dust with not a single tree in sight, they found at last, says Samuel, 'a beautiful spring of water about 300 yards south of the road near a marsh'. This was 'the well-known spring' that Francis Parkman in his *The Oregon Trail* (1846) describes as appearing just in time to breathe new life into battered humans and animals. The spring bubbled opposite the historic Scott's Bluff, a name to be remembered in the saga of the opening-up of the American West by the trappers of beaver, especially when admired from the north side of the stream where the Cornish were camping. In the evening light the bluffs stood 'majestic and sublime' (as Clayton discribes them), tinted with the most delicate shades of pink, perhaps recalling that golden glow on the ancient granite cliffs of the Lizard in Cornwall as the sun sank beneath the sea's horizon. John Rogers remembered thankfully that 'the clear dry atmosphere, bright starlight night and the dry roads and generally comfortable camping places were great things for the emigrant'. And no doubt William Carson Stone in the cool and stillness of the evening told his version of the tragic story of Scott, the young trapper-clerk who worked for the American Fur Company some thirty years earlier, and who was abandoned by his companions and left to die on the bluffs where his bleached skeleton was found some years later.[9]

The first day of June was a Sunday, normally for the Cornish a sacred day on the trail, but sometimes the Sabbath could not be observed for practical reasons, and this was the case now, because Samuel wanted to push on with all speed to Fort Laramie about 50 miles from Scott's Bluff. So on this Sunday Johnson the preacher sacrificed his sermon, but donned his silk hat and made do with a few prayers and readings from the Bible, standing in his one-horse buggy as usual with his wife by his side (the buggy later disintegrated in the Cascade Mountains). That night, after 21 miles of burning sun, they finally camped at Spring Creek, their exhaustion forgotten by the sight of trout, wild sunflowers, lavender and daisies adorning what Samuel described as 'an interesting rock country resembling some fine scenery in Old England'. One more march of 25 miles through Mitchell's Pass and they were within four miles of the fort, the first perhaps to come that way, for the other pass through these badlands, Robidoux Pass, appears to have been abandoned the previous year.[10]

NOTES

1. Merrill J. Mattes, *The Great Platte River Road*, p. 139.
2. Ibid., p. 132.
3. Ibid., p. 241.
4. Ibid., p. 43.
5. Ibid., p. 37.
6. For more information see Merrill J. Mattes, 'Chimney Rock on the Oregon Trail', *Nebraska History* 36, March 1955, pp. 1–26. For a contemporary impression see back cover of this book.
7. Merrill J. Mattes, *The Great Platte River Road*, p. 383.
8. Ibid., pp. 84, 85.
9. For a detailed account of the tragedy of Scott's Bluff, see ibid., pp. 426–35.
10. Ibid., p. 436.

CHAPTER 6

Fort Laramie to the Continental Divide

Built in 1834 by Robert Campbell and William Sublette with high adobe walls surmounted by a wooden palisade and a massive main entrance of two gates linked by an arched passage, Fort Laramie was originally a trading post in a rich trapping area and was named after a Canadian trapper, one Jacques La Ramee. It belonged to the American Fur Company who sold it to the US Government in 1849. It was the most welcome of sights to the jaded Cornish as their wagons lumbered and squeaked to a halt in the billowing dust on 3 June 1851, for it was garrisoned by federal troops for the express purpose of giving aid and succour to emigrants. This had necessitated making a treaty of friendship with the Sioux and Cheyennes who could be seen in semi-permanent occupation in their tepees just outside the fort. In return for allowing the emigrants to pass unmolested through their lands the Indians were for three years paid the equivalent of fifty thousand dollars a year. As 1851 was the first year of this payment, Samuel and his companions found the Indians unusually friendly, even though they had a reputation for not being unduly hostile, some Europeans even marrying into their tribes. John Rogers reports that his family camped outside the fort, right in the middle of the Indians, and at once liked them. The red men patted themselves on the chest and said, 'Me good Indian', and gave them to understand that they were not like the Pawnees. Attracted by the huge tanned buffalo skin tents, John Rogers went 'peeking in' at the opening and saw strings of buffalo meat hanging up and drying in the smoke of a fire built in the middle of the tent. A 'large mother-looking squaw with great wide tanned leather skirts that spread away out' took him by the hand and was showing him round the tent when his mother came up hurriedly and grabbed him 'from the opposite side of the big skirts'. But he continued to admire these Indians as the 'finest looking lot' he ever saw, for they stood up 'tall and straight and manly looking, full of life and anxious to make trades'.

There were not many travellers to crowd the fort in 1851, and nothing like the numbers appearing on the register for the previous year: 37,171 men, 803 women, 1,094 children and 8,988 wagons.[1] But there was little time for more than essential bargains, Samuel spending no more than a single day at the fort, so anxious was he to be away, now that he had put some 500 miles behind them since leaving Kanesville. But before they pulled out, they were amazed and hilariously surprised to see being driven into the stockade the very prized ox they thought they had lost the week before. It is likely to have been afforded a special shout of welcome, especially by the children. So, with new supplies on board and the ox reclaimed, the small train moved out in the knowledge that Fort Laramie marked the end of the high plains and the start of the long haul to the crests of the Rocky Mountains. Samuel knew that this new section of the trail was more rugged than any they had yet faced and, as if to reinforce that knowledge, before them boldly stood, forty miles away, Laramie Peak, their first view of the Rocky Mountains ahead of them.

As yet the terrain west of the fort filled them with sheer delight. Their first camp was some eight miles out in the Black Hills in a high meadow which Samuel christened Pasture Grove because he thought it a 'beautiful place, delightful country, fit for angels to dwell in', as he recorded on 4 June. In fact from now onwards all the streams and plants he mentions in his journal were named by him.[2] Pasture Grove indeed was a paradise of nature, where grew in profusion mountain cherry, wild roses, blue flax and larkspur. The evening air was vibrant with the heady fragrance of pine, cedar and sage in the smoke that spiralled from the evening fires, and in the morning on waking they breathed an air so pure that they must have felt equal to any agonies and obstacles that might stand in the path.

They needed a resurgence of confidence for this paradise proved bitterly deceptive. The Black Hills were deep and savage cuts in the land, each following the other over wild wind-swept ridges at an exhausting altitude of 7000 feet, from where rain, frost and wild winds had dislodged sharp rocks that littered the trail, splitting the hooves of the animals and puncturing the feet of children. It was here that the real troubles of emigrants began, the military having usually warned them in vain never to tackle these hills in small parties. It was not only that the hills were 'grim', as Parkman remarked, but many emigrants tended to be foolhardy. After their arrival at the fort, tired and dispirited from their daily battle with the sand and water of the Platte, they invariably overloaded their wagons with fresh supplies for the Wyoming stretch of the trail, only to find that they could not carry the burdens.

Samuel, always a meticulous planner, and his family are hardly likely to have made such serious errors of judgement. Thus they were able to reduce the chances of serious accidents that affected other parties: shootings, drownings, being crushed under wagon wheels, broken limbs, bodily mutilations, severed thumbs, smashed skulls, and the like. Nevertheless, on 5 June, the day after they left Pasture Grove, Samuel's wagons ran into serious trouble as the oxen strained to pull their loads through the mud and sodden soils of the river bottoms. In one day they only managed five miles and, according to John Rogers, at Clear Creek 'a wagon broke in pieces', a calamity that defies the imagination. Was it a total wreck? Could any parts be salvaged? Was the wood kept as a reserve for firing to help them to survive in a land where wood was almost non-existent? Abandoned wagon tyres were a common sight. They were usually left by Indians who carried off what remained of the wooden skeletons of derelict wagons after their owners had written them off as a total loss. Immense volcanic fissures split the plains and hills of Wyoming, and when Samuel's boys found a tyre they would drop it into one of the cracks, hoping to estimate its depth. The trails too were littered with the remains of unwanted kitchen equipment, small stoves, pots, pans and kettles. John Rogers even found an English turning-spit for roasting beef. More tragic were lonely graves, often with the dead one's clothing left alongside the fresh-dug sand and stones. He remembered the grave of one young man, his heavy overcoat still moving in the afternoon breeze from a stake driven in the ground. It was said that Indians were fearful of going near these graves and so would not molest them.

Though we do not know the fate of Samuel's wagon, the party seems to have been luckier on 6 June, for they found an inexhaustible supply of fresh water at Box Elder Creek, where they 'nooned', and in the evening camped by another stream which Samuel named Wayside Creek. A 'run' of 21 miles under a blinding sun on 7 June, with no water for miles, seems to have passed without incident, though all were beginning to feel the weakening effects of toiling through a land that was drearily sandy, arid and broken, and along a trail that forced them painfully, slowly and breathlessly to ever higher altitudes in an intense summer heat. Robert Louis Stevenson, like Samuel, expected that the mountains of Wyoming would provide a welcome relief from the dry plains of Nebraska. But even from the comfort of the observation car of a Union Pacific train (which he describes in 1892 in his *Across the Plains*), Stevenson was compelled to despair of the misery of the aspect, the tumbled boulders, cliffs 'that dreamily imitated the shape of mountains and fortifications,' the lack of trees, the perpetual gloomy colouring of greys and browns, the eternal sage-brush, and the only sign of life, a fleeting antelope. Samuel actually managed to shoot one and soon learned not to despise the sage-brush, for it was now their only source of firing, though never so good a retainer of heat as the buffalo chip.

The next 50 miles ahead were to be the most gruelling and testing of the whole journey so far. To begin with they floundered, according to Samuel's journal, through 'very rough hilly country' with 'hard travelling over high hills' and 'very heavy sandy roads' which lamed some of the oxen. Lameness in cattle was always a worry but especially in Wyoming, where a low ground-covering of cactus bedevilled both man and beast. Samuel's practice was to carry spares of oxen half-shoes which he nailed on each side of the cloven hoof; this usually cured and prevented further lameness. On 12 June, knowing the nature of the next ordeal, he 'concluded to rest today previous to taking a long drive through an alkali country' and was much comforted when he spotted a flight of magpies, in Cornwall the harbingers of good luck, provided you touched the forelock as a mark of reverence. Certainly they needed every scrap of luck to survive this alkali desert, scorched, baked hard and pocked with stagnant pools covered with the black scum of copper deposits, soda and sulphur that exuded an evil smell like rotting eggs or bad drains. It made everyone feel nauseated. They could not keep food down in their stomachs. They retched and vomited and so added to the filth and stench on the trail, all the while needing to keep their red and itching eyes on the cattle lest they should drink the poisoned water, for if they did they would surely die a horrible death unless fed with fat pork. To make matters worse fierce winds blew the alkali dust into everyone's eyes, ears and nostrils, and the red sun completed the misery by baking the deposits hard on their already tender skin. Cheeks would peel and lips split open.[3] 'No good water on the way', complained Samuel. And yet, at the end of this seemingly never-ending sanded wasteland, the oxen would first smell, and then their drivers would dimly see, the bright white ribbon of the Sweetwater River, a beautiful mountain stream of swift, clean clear water.

On 13 June the spirits of all rose when there slowly grew out of the desert, so it seemed, the impressive Independence Rock which they had been told to look out for. Supposedly named by a party of trappers of the American Fur Company who arrived there on 4 July 1824,[4] it looked to some like a gigantic misshapen loaf of bread, standing alone on the plain, unattached to any other geological formation, a solid monolithic upthrust of grey granite that must have reminded the Cornish so much of their own homeland. It was 650 yards long, 280 yards wide, and 193 feet high at the north end and 167 feet at the south end, almost a mile in circumference and enclosed an area of 38 acres. John Rogers wrote that it stood 'lonely and grand' and looked 'like the biggest rock in existence, as big as a city block two or three stories high'. As they drew nearer and were dwarfed by its sheer size, they could see that its base was covered with the names of earlier pioneers who had passed that way. John Rogers tells us that his brother Samuel on whom the elder Samuel depended so much throughout the journey and of whom we hear too little, was so excited by this 'Great Register of the Desert',[5] that he picked up the bucket of tar that was used for greasing the axles and with a brush began to daub their names on the rocky surface. His mother, no doubt thinking that the precious tar would be needed later, angrily exclaimed: 'Fools' names, like their faces, are always seen in public places.' The doggerel was not lost on her husband who retorted, 'no fool would venture so far from civilisation'.[6]

Some six miles south-west of the Rock, another geological landmark awaited them, the Devil's Gate, a deep cleft in a rock face that had been worn away by the Sweetwater River, producing a gorge some four hundred feet deep.[7] As the river flowed eastwards to empty itself in the Platte, the gate it had cut through the living rock seemed to be *the* gateway to the west, especially when the emigrants had passed through and looked back. John Rogers thought it the entrance to paradise itself for they saw laid out before them, like a carpet, water meadows of wild flowers and grasses that seemed to move in the wind upwards to the tops of every slope. 'They were a delight to our weary eyes, and we were refreshed in both body and mind', he wrote, revelling in the keen air of the Green Mountains at a height of six thousand feet above the level of the sea from which these Cornish had come. The Sweetwater, only about 40 yards wide and three feet deep, was to be their travelling companion for the next 100 miles and the best part of a week. Its bottom was sandy, its current strong and it twisted and meandered every quarter of a mile or so, much like the first bearer of that name in ancient Troy. One of today's authorities on the Oregon Trail, Clyde Arbuckle of San José in California, who has many times followed on foot the waywardness of the river, says that the Sweetwater River is the most notable study in hydrographic sinuosity he has ever seen and doubts that it flows straight for 30 feet in any stretch of its course. John Rogers thought it 'must be a wicked torrent in winter' for he and his brothers climbed to the top of the cliff and looked down into 'the foaming roaring stream below'. They came down quickly when they found signs of blood in a basin in the rocks. They walked in the stream to cool themselves, as did the cattle, but soon gave up because of the extra ground they had to cover. And leaving the water for the trail was hardly an improvement as Samuel commented on Sunday 15 June: 'Road now all granite and gravel, hard on cattle's feet, many lame'. Six miles of such agony constituted enough suffering for all God's creatures on the day usually set aside for rest and prayer.

But Samuel was captivated and entranced by the new look of the land, particularly by the sage-brush, the *artemesis tridentata* that grew to a height of almost 10 feet and spread its dull grey and dusty coloured carpet as far as the eye could see, exuding a fragrance that he never forgot. Along the river too grew an abundance of bunch or buffalo grass, dry in June, which the cattle preferred to munch rather than the greener grass that billowed from the river's edge. But this profusion covered hidden dangers, and a warning soon came. A 'lone traveller', leading a saddle pony, rode into camp and introduced himself as a volunteer 'express' mail carrier who had been entrusted with letters from business men and army officers to deliver to post offices on the Missouri River for onward transmission east. Part Indian, he spoke excellent English and said that he charged 50 cents per letter. Samuel immediately took advantage of this surprising service and wrote to his relatives in Cornwall, in spite of a warning from his wife that this was the last he would see of both the letter and the 50 cents. But he was more than justified by his faith in the courier for John Rogers records that a reply from Cornwall actually reached them in Oregon Territory some months later.

Before he continued his ride east the wandering mailman warned Samuel of the dangers lurking in the dense undergrowth of sage-brush and greasewood (a prickly plant that grew in alkaline soils) because it provided perfect cover for the 'treacherous' Crow Indians. So, from now onwards, Samuel took extra precautions at sundown, corraling the cattle, forming the wagons into a defensive square, and posting more guards. But they saw no Indians, only the pillars of smoke to the north towering as high as the clouds, which were signal fires made by the Crows who were either hunting or waging war on the Blackfoot Indians. With that danger successfully avoided, the young boy John Rogers and his family apparently found time to enjoy the trail and 'the many things of interest on the way' because 'the dusty, sandy, rocky, sage-brush plains with the pure air and plenty of exercise makes us appreciate the beauties of Nature'. And, as he saw in the far distance the Wind River range of mountains, he declared enthusiastically: 'The lofty white peaks seemed to impress me with a supernatural vision: the towering peaks, piercing, pointing everlastingly to the heavens, bore witness to the ages past and unknown future to come.'

Between Independence Rock and the Wind River lay another 100 miles of exceptionally rugged country that they knew would bring them to the most significant of all geographical landmarks, the Continental Divide. It proved a nightmare of a journey through a land of desolation and death. On 16 June Samuel scrawled in his journal: 'Bitter Cottonwood Creek, alkali, bones of cattle whiten all the way.' The next day, at a ford of the Sweetwater, they 'passed a horrid canyon and a country full of poison' where, according to his son, 'we found the carcasses of many oxen, and the wayside streams had the bones of cattle which had died years before.'

By now the emigrant train had become scattered, only five, six, eight or ten wagons ever grouped together. They were working their way to the summit of South Pass through the southern end of the Wind River range of the Rocky Mountains which, said the guide-books, was not particularly difficult to negotiate. Indeed the pass was about eighty miles long and twenty miles wide, the gradient so gradual as to be hardly perceptible, and the summit flat and unbroken. Yet it presented the tired travellers with new problems. None of them had any experience of the weakening effect of exerting themselves at altitudes of almost eight thousand feet, of manhandling wagons and encouraging the nigh exhausted cattle that somehow had managed to survive. It was bad enough to contend with giddiness, headaches and mountain sickness, but at that altitude the air was piercingly cold and even in June they would have found themselves floundering in drifts of summer snow.

Between two and three miles from the summit of South Pass they parted with the Sweetwater. Samuel, ever sensitive to the drama of the occasion, observed that they were now leaving the last connecting link with their native land, namely the Sweetwater River, which flowed into the Mississippi, thence into the Gulf of Mexico and, driven by cross currents, dashed its billows on the cliffs of Cornwall. John Rogers recalled how rocky the road was to the summit and how the jolting and lurching and bouncing of the wagons were so violent and sickening that his mother was forced to walk the last mile or so. Wrapped in her shawl to keep out the cold and breathing hard in the crisp rare air, he saw her clinging to his father's arm for support. On 19 June they saw 'daisies and beautiful scented flowers' along 'the road [which was] level and smooth and broad, of granite gravel'. Samuel took out his sextant (the first time he mentions it) and with a flourish recorded their position: 'Altitude 7085 feet, Latitude 42° 18′ 48″ N, Longitude 108° 40′ W'. He was a little hasty for he was not yet quite at the summit, having still to climb to the Continental Divide watershed, but, as far as we know, his was the first Cornish family to have reached this altitude, and Samuel the first Cornish emigrant to have guided family, wagons and cattle there without loss. Even his load of books was intact after their true *gradus ad Parnassum*.

The next day, 20 June, after floundering through the last alkali swamp, they 'went through the great South Pass and drank out of Pacific Springs', the very first stream, Samuel reminded his family, they had seen flowing westwards. They celebrated by paring away some of their stale Iowa sausage, now 'getting a little strong', munching hard tack and 'getting down on our stomachs and drinking from these springs'. So, with the mountain streams now flowing westwards, giving the impression of speeding them on their way to Oregon, they were still feeling somewhat light-headed as they began their long descent. And time was on their side. July 4 was reckoned a good date to have arrived at the Continental Divide, so Samuel was two weeks ahead of schedule.

NOTES

1. Merrill J. Mattes, *The Great Platte River Road*, p. 503.
2. Entry for 11 June 1851.
3. Gregory M. Franzwa, *The Oregon Trail Revisited* (Patrice Press, St Louis, Missouri, 2nd edition, 1978), p. 41.
4. Ibid., p. 258.
5. This description seems to have been first used by Pierre-Jean DeSmet, the Jesuit missionary to Oregon, in 1841. See Franzwa, pp. 20–1.
6. See Robert S. Ellison, *Independence Rock, The Great Register of the Desert* (Caspar, Wyoming, Natrona County Historical Society, 1930), 41 pp.
7. Franzwa, pp. 262–4.

CHAPTER 7

From the Continental Divide to Raft River

The early morning of 21 June appeared pleasant enough as the wagons rolled along gentle slopes covered with 'some pretty flowers which we had not seen before', as John Rogers noticed. Walking with the lead team and reaching the brow of a hill overlooking 'a large scope of country to the West', he was elated and astonished, as were the others, to see 'pictures in the heavens, a river bright and clear, wandering through a border of trees, with streams on either side, plains and hills in the background'.

It was a mirage for they were only too aware of the frightening reality of the next desert that awaited them, a daunting 52 miles over a baked and waterless plain to Green River. But first they had to grapple with the Dry Sandy River, a watercourse that marked the parting of the ways, for here the wagon-trains bound for California (and Oregon originally) took a south-westerly route to Fort Bridger. It was the longest day of the year and they were locked in a notorious 'barren country'[1] where even the streams were brackish and oxen lay down to die, the stench from their putrifying carcasses sickening travellers already weakened to the point of collapse by dehydration and the unbelievably unbearable sun. From the Dry Sandy they struggled to the Little Sandy, the oxen now barely heeding the crack of the teamsters' whips as they searched for the so-called Sublette cut-off to Green River. This historic road, now nearly obliterated and the subject of controversy, was used in the 1840s to reach Fort Hall by Oregon-bound trains, especially that led in 1844 by Caleb Greenwood, whose name often appeared on contemporary maps of the region until Andrew Sublette used the route. Joseph E. Ware in his *The Emigrant's Guide to California* of 1849, which Samuel may have used, says that he 'took the liberty' of calling the route Sublette's Cut-off, and so it must have been in Samuel's time. It began near the Little Sandy in present Wyoming, hit the Big Sandy and then continued 35 miles across the desert to Green River. For this notorious stretch of the trail Samuel's roadmeter measured $32\frac{1}{2}$ miles which shows that his party is likely to have been travelling on the original road, no matter who discovered it.

The Oregon Trail at Little Sandy, Wyoming. Photograph Helen Arbuckle, San José, California

It was on Sunday 22 June, again no day of rest and with the summer sun almost overhead, that Samuel and his drivers braked their wagons down the mountain to the Big Sandy, where they rested in preparation for the only possible time for traversing the desert, by night. Having loaded up with several barrels of water from the Big Sandy, they slowly snaked their way by a succession of alkaline lakes, sandy depressions and rocky hills. John Rogers described this night drive as 'not bad', no doubt on account of the clear skies, the brilliance of the stars, the coolness of the desert and the unusual experience of actually wandering through the stillness of the night. Just before dawn they stopped to refresh the cattle with the now brackish and stinking water from the barrels and then staggered resolutely into a day which was to be 'distressing for both man and beast'. As the morning advanced, the searing heat thrown up from the baking earth and hurled down from the unpropitiated sun, and the scorching wind that shot the stinging sand in eyes, ears and nostrils, made the final 20 miles to Green River a howling hell. To falter and stop for a single moment was suicidal for here indeed was the point of no return, where cold leadership and cool nerves were needed to survive. Samuel reports no losses, not even of a single book.

Before them aimlessly rambled the Green River, 'magnificent looking, deep and swift, not fordable', rendezvous of many a trapping party years before.

About 150 yards wide and 10 feet deep, it was still as green in colour as when first discovered by the Spaniards. But long before it could be seen, the parched oxen would have sniffed its waters, lunging and pulling on the traces in a frantic effort to reach it before they collapsed. To prevent a stampede, Samuel tells us, the teamsters stopped the wagons about half a mile from the river, unyoked the oxen and left them to stagger down the bluffs to the river. Yet, ever fearful of water, they ventured no further than the edge and then drank until their sides were so swollen that it seemed as if they must surely burst, though Lucas assured Samuel they would come to no harm as long as they stood with all four feet in the water. John Rogers and his parents, his brothers and sisters threw themselves down on their stomachs and drank, 'their necks stretched out like geese'.

The river still had to be crossed and on the west bank a Mormon detachment was already in position with the one and only ferry to make it possible. It consisted of a boat propelled by a static rope made of chains normally used for logging and which had been welded together and bound with deer skins to ensure the smooth running of the chain over a set of pulleys. Normally Samuel would have shown interest in the contrivance, but he was annoyed at the fee to be paid, as much as ten dollars a wagon. But there seemed no point in arguing, for the Mormons were supported by a sizeable party of Shoshone Indians to enforce their demands.

Though the passage through the country immediately ahead was not likely to be as tough as that they had just left, there were hazards. On 24 June, midsummer day, Samuel recorded '8 miles Fontanelle Creek', his only comment on the slow ascent of the bluffs to the plateau through which flowed the stream named after Lucian Fontanelle, once chief factor of the American Fur Company. The next day, 25 June, only five miles were covered, and they spent the night near a spring under a thick border of willow trees at the foot of a bluff. Another 15 miles of the same rough and tiring tediousness brought them to the approaches to another mountain, thick with clumps of stunted fir and ravaged with ravines and canyons. Of this 20-mile ascent and descent of stumbling and sweating agony Samuel wrote on 27 June: 'Went over a very high sidling hill, one of my wagons upset'. The accident was probably the consequence of too rapid a descent to the spacious valley of Ham's Fork where Samuel anticipated a welcome of fresh water and bunch grass. On 28 June they crossed Smith's Fork which perpetuated the memory of the celebrated Jedediah Smith who in 1826 made the first crossing of the Mojave Desert into California, and then 'after a dreadful rocky road between high cliffs' they entered a valley of the Bear River. This must have seemed a gift from God with its lush knee-deep grass, fresh water, fish, elk and antelope, friendly Shoshones and unlimited wood for firing. Sunday 29 June therefore came as a day for restful thanksgiving, and culminated with 'a sermon preached by a Mr Johnson from near New London, Iowa'.

On 30 June they crossed the present Wyoming line into Idaho and forded the

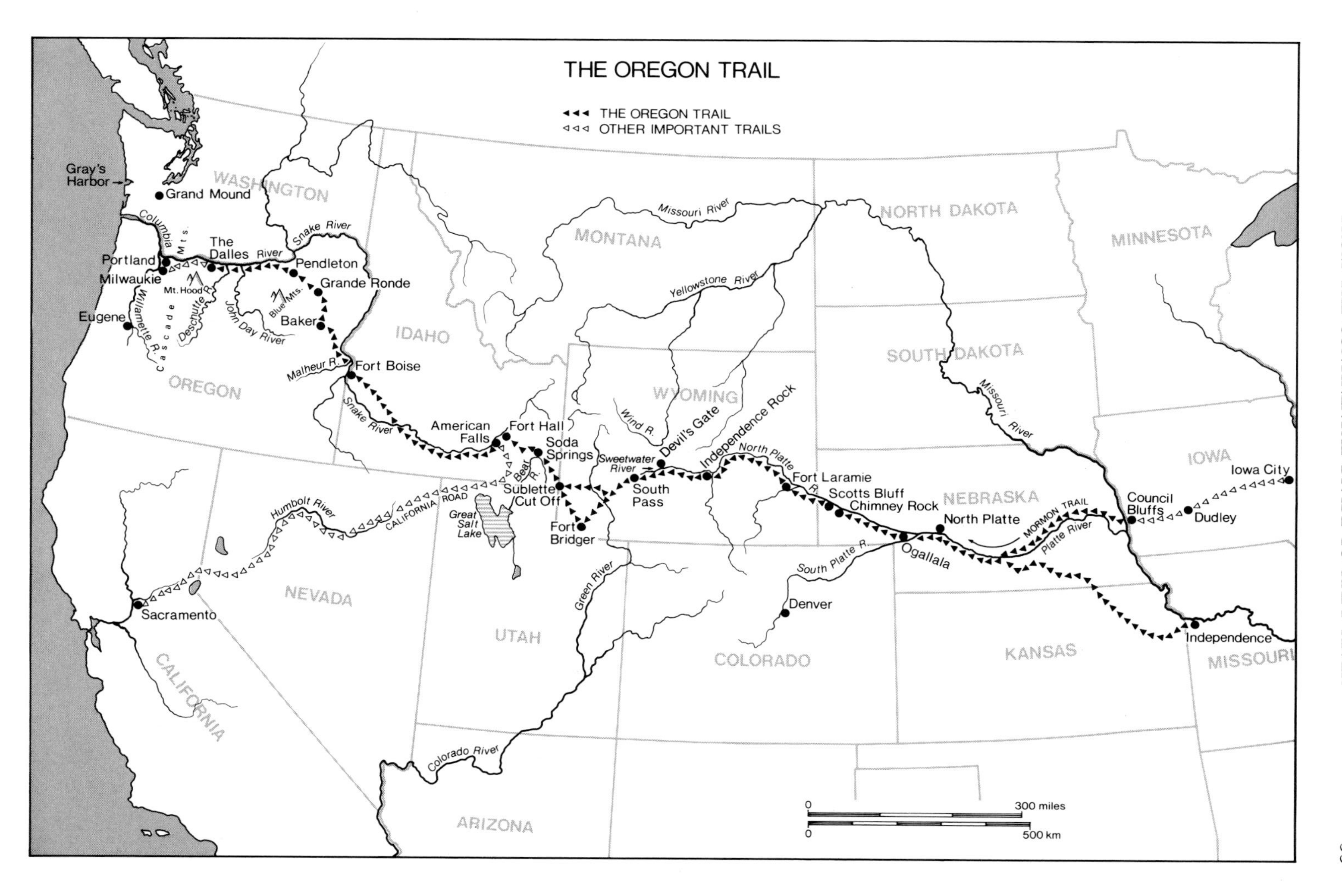
THE OREGON TRAIL
THE OREGON TRAIL
OTHER IMPORTANT TRAILS
Gray's Harbor
Grand Mound
WASHINGTON
Columbia
Mts.
Portland
Milwaukie
The Dalles
River
Snake River
Pendleton
Grande Ronde
Mt. Hood
Blue Mts.
Baker
Eugene
Willamette R.
Cascade
Deschutte R.
John Day River
IDAHO
Malheur R.
Fort Boise
OREGON
Snake River
American Falls
Fort Hall
Soda Springs
Beat R.
Sublette Cut Off
Fort Bridger
MONTANA
Missouri River
Yellowstone River
WYOMING
Wind R.
Sweetwater River
Devil's Gate
Independence Rock
South Pass
North Platte R.
Fort Laramie
Scotts Bluff
Chimney Rock
NORTH DAKOTA
SOUTH DAKOTA
Missouri River
MINNESOTA
IOWA
Iowa City
Council Bluffs
Dudley
NEBRASKA
North Platte
MORMON TRAIL
Platte River
Ogallala
South Platte R.
Denver
Independence
KANSAS
MISSOURI
COLORADO
Green River
UTAH
Great Salt Lake
CALIFORNIA ROAD
Humbolt River
NEVADA
Sacramento
CALIFORNIA
Colorado River
ARIZONA
0 300 miles
0 500 km

straggling Thomas Fork River with some difficulty, encountering strong currents racing through deep cuts in the rock. Two more days were consumed at an elevation of some 6000 feet in hacking a way through what has since been called Emigrant Canyon with mountain masses pressing on them from either side, and then in traversing a long prairie of the Bear River (the Union Pacific Railroad follows closely their route) until 3 July when they arrived at Soda Springs. Samuel was exhilarated because the ground was covered with blackened stones and the earth split open by steaming springs bursting in jets from lava beds below. It was, he wrote 'a wonderful place of recently extinguished volcanoes', though John Rogers contented himself with remarking that it was very 'cosy looking'. On 4 July, with the Soda Spring Hills to their right, and another wasteland still to cross, they struggled over two more creeks and finally forded the Portneuf River, where they apparently still had enough reserve of energy and enthusiasm not to forget Independence Day for it was here that they 'fired a grand salute', drank a few toasts in coffee and rested for the final push to their next objective. So on 5 July, still at a heady elevation of 6000 feet, they 'crossed summit of hill between Bear River and Fort Hall', and faced another 40 miles of desert to reach the fort.

This famous fort had been established as a trading post in 1834 by Nathaniel Wyeth of Boston, but in 1836 was bought by the Hudson's Bay Company to assist emigrants on their way to the Pacific North-West. The first factor was John Day but, when the Cornish arrived, Samuel found that Day's son was in charge, a shiftless loafer born to Day's Shoshone wife. John Rogers says that they soon found that he was completely untrustworthy and so they preferred to camp outside the fort on a bank of the Snake River where the boys could practise 'wading and trying to swim from one bank to the other'. His mother too complained bitterly about the excessive prices Day charged, for instance half a dollar for a fine tooth comb, though one supposes there must have been strong demand considering the state of their hair.

Day's Indian 'friends' proved less than friendly. Samuel awoke one morning to find that his cattle had been rustled. Some were recovered but 'Old Dave', his heaviest and strongest ox, lay dead in the river. Robert Foster, however, was robbed of his entire team. 'There stood the wagon, wife and children, helpless in wilderness, a lonely looking prospect' until his neighbours fitted them up with a makeshift team. So they all hurriedly left the vicinity of Fort Hall to the taunts of the Indians on the bluffs across the river who bending over, defied them to shoot them in the back-sides, knowing full well that they were outside the range of their muzzle-loading rifles.[2] Perhaps it is hardly surprising that, since Day never really met the needs of the emigrants, the fort was abandoned in 1856.[3]

The 7th of July saw the voyagers some two miles west of the fort. Samuel reported ripening wheat and 'immense quantities of large black crickets'. On 8 July they were almost within sight and sound of the American Falls, where the Snake writhes its spectacular way through a precipitous gorge of basalt, only to discover that the Indians had struck again. 'One of my oxen killed', lamented Samuel, 'the day spent in pursuing the marauders but without success'. By 11 July they had pushed on by overbearing mountain masses to the fork of the Raft River, another historic spot for it was here, as Samuel notes, that 'the Californian road branches'. It was indeed the very last parting of the ways, the right-handed turn to Oregon, and the left-hand to California along the Applegate Trail.[4] Here son Thomas, only 13 but hardened by life on the trail, paused for a momentous decision. He was intrigued, recalled John Rogers, by the golden opportunities in mining that California offered when talking to a group of emigrants who were going there. John Rogers tells us that their father watched this and then went over and had a serious talk with Tom, who decided not to part company but to continue on to Oregon.

NOTES

1. Journal of Samuel James, 21 June 1851.
2. Autobiography of John Rogers James (1916).
3. Irene D. Paden, *The Wake of the Prairie Schooner* (Macmillan, New York, 1943), p. 279; and Aubrey L. Haines, *Historic Sites Along the Oregon Trail* (Patrice Press, Gerald, Missouri, 1981), pp. 293–305. See also Jennie Broughton Brown, *Fort Hall on the Oregon Trail* (Caldwell, Idaho, Caxton Printers, 1932), 466 pp.
4. The Applegate Trail was named after Jesse Applegate who in 1846 led a large party of 120 wagons and a huge herd of cattle to California. See Walter E. Meacham, *Applegate Trail* (Portland, Oregon, 1947), 26 pp.

CHAPTER 8

The Road to Oregon

Following the course of the Snake River northwards seemed a simple matter, but Samuel found that this waterway differed considerably from the ones to which they had been accustomed. It was constantly disappearing from view for it could only be seen from the tops of gorges several hundreds of feet deep. The plunging river below teamed with nourishing fish but, paradoxically, on the summits of these basaltic gorges there was neither fish nor water. Not only was it an unmapped and sun-cracked landscape of despair, but the oxen had to be driven dangerously near to the very brink of the gorge in order to keep in sight the life-sustaining and direction-finding river that was forever tantalisingly out of reach. On 12 July Samuel logged 20 miles of this torture of 'no water for 16 miles'. The next main objective, Salmon Falls, lay some 60 miles farther north and this meant at least five more days of struggle across 'bad desert'.[1] They had experienced plenty of that ordeal before but in Idaho, because of the height of gorges above the river, they were afflicted by a perplexing nausea and dizziness. Sky, cliffs and river all seemed to spin around them in an unpleasant vortex of confused sight and sound.

Where the city of Twin Falls now stands, they encountered at Rock Creek a vast chasm of columnar rock—called a 'zawn' in Cornwall. At first sight the crossing of the creek seemed not too difficult for it was only 20 feet wide. But the rock had to be circumvented before they could begin a steep and fearsome descent to the crossing place, and here the waters boiled in a frenzied turbulence of noise, stirred by the many falls that spouted from fissures in the basaltic rock. There was little time for reflecting on the translucent beauty of the Shoshone Falls, their cool-clean spray and the magic of the rainbows, for they were all anxious to cover the next 30 miles as speedily as possible to the most spectacular of all falls, the Upper Salmon Falls. The Snake, they will have found, now bounded forward, as if carrying the voyagers with it, for it drops no less than 70 feet in one and a half miles, giving the illusion of wagons plunging forward and as if without their loads. But at Upper Salmon Falls the Snake was wider and calmer than they had expected to see it and full of fish. Here in deep caves on the high banks of the river lived Indians who were considered the friendliest of people until the first emigrants from the east appeared who naturally helped themselves liberally to the fish. The Indians, however, properly regarded the fish as their very own private property, so they retaliated by helping themselves to the white man's cattle.

By the time the Cornish appeared on the scene, the red man's hostility was evident. On 17 July Samuel wrote: 'Indians very bad—one man shot'. John Rogers noted that his father was especially worried by one Indian who wandered into their camp, stayed a night and a day, and then disappeared. Wise to Indian ways, William Stone warned Samuel that this meant that an attack was imminent. As they moved through a narrow defile cut by the Snake, Stone saw the face of an Indian peering round a bush. The entire train was halted and Samuel ordered his teamsters to charge with loaded guns in the direction of the bush. The Indians then made off on their ponies only to return riding in circles round the wagons. Samuel had 'an old big fellow' in his sights and would have opened fire but for a sudden jolt to his conscience: 'I will never take the life of a human being unless compelled'. But it had been a dangerous situation as they discovered shortly afterwards, when they came across a party of fellow emigrants who had been forced to stop because an Indian had shot one of their men through the bowels. Samuel and John Rogers saw the victim lying on his bed in the wagon in dreadful agony. His wife explained that he had gone down to the river for water and had run into an ambush. John Rogers was shocked for 'this was the first bullet wound I had seen'. The man never recovered.[2]

For the next ten days Samuel and his companions had to contend not only with hostile Indians, but also with an unfriendly landscape of gulches (ravines) that never once relented for 130 miles, as his journal shows: '18 July, no water on the way, horrible place, no grass'. Worse followed on 24 July: 'Currant Creek, the most desolate country in the whole world, the region of the shadow of death'. On 25 July they travelled for 16 miles and again found no water. The following day they encountered 'hot springs, running water as clear as crystal and hot enough to scald'. Samuel was so preoccupied with the difficulties of the trail that he does not seem to have been at all sure of the direction in which he was travelling. For instance, he makes no mention of the formidable maze of the Three Island Crossing, whether he was able to cross the Snake or whether he continued on the south side of the river to a point in Oregon just west of Fort Boise.[3] We do know, however, that he reached Fort Boise[4] on 29 July and that he successfully crossed the Owyhee River on the same day, gratified that at last they were treading the soil of Oregon. The next day brought another river to ford, the well-named Malheur, at the point where it plunged into the Snake. It was a river of hot springs that brought no respite from the insufferable heat that clung to the bottoms of the canyons. For 43 miles its path lay through dead empty desolate hills. The end of July brought more alkali springs, so many that they 'nooned at a sulphur spring', ironically called Birch Creek, whose water was undrinkable.

On the first day of August yet another crossing loomed ahead, Burnt River, described by Samuel as 'a bad place to be attacked by Indians and much dreaded', though John Rogers thought them more than friendly. A solitary Indian would appear on his pony and, when a little way off, would hold up both hands and cross his forefingers. This meant that he wanted to trade for stale hard-tack, bread and old strong sausage. What he had to offer in exchange was *lacamas*, a species of onion which could be steam-cooked on the hot rocks and then served as a delicacy, as indeed it was after eating indigestible dried salmon for days on end.[5] On 2 August a 20-mile thrust brought Samuel to the head of Burnt River through 'a very bad narrow wooded valley all stoney between high mountains', probably Bald Mountain (6883 feet) to the west and Dooley Mountain (5392 feet) to the east. Almost facing them rose the 4000 foot summit of the headwaters of the Burnt and Powder rivers that watered a beautiful valley of lush pasture ('excellent grass', commented Samuel) and opened a way into a second valley, but only after conquering ' a terrible hill' over which 'most of the drivers quaked in getting their wagons down'.

This welcoming valley greeted them on 6 August. It was watered by the Grande Ronde River or 'Grand Round' as these Cornish-Americans pronounced it. As far as their tired eyes could see, right to the foothills of the Blue Mountains in the west, billowed a sea of grass. Trees grew in abundance along the margins of numberless streams. It was, said Samuel, with unerring instinct 'a most beautiful site for a farm . . . an enchanting place, the best of land, grass and water'. John Rogers declared that any emigrant arriving here might have 'gone right to work ploughing the rich black soil'.[6] Indeed this was the place where was to grow the city of La Grande. But in 1851 the valley was hardly the place for white settlement, being the battle ground of two hostile tribes, the Cayuse from the west and the Shoshones from the east. Luckily Samuel's party saw no signs of either and they were able to rest for two days in preparation for their crossing of the Blue Mountains, much dreaded because heavily timbered with tall pine, fir and hemlock. Of this trial of strength and patience Samuel only refers briefly but pointedly: 'Over a mighty hill in the Blue Mountains'. But once through the pass, the rolling plains of east Oregon greeted them and, near the Umatilla River, Samuel again did not fail to notice the 'most excellent land' for farming, while 150 miles away in the west he could actually see the snow-covered peaks of the Cascades. Beyond them, he knew, lay their final destination, the valley of the Willamette River.

The major difficulties and perils of the long journey from Wisconsin were perhaps by now becoming a faint memory. Yet Samuel was alert enough to realise that they were still travelling through enemy country, that of the Cayuse Indians who roamed the area now occupied by the modern city of Pendleton. In 1847 they had massacred the Whitman missionary family and their chiefs had been hanged just a year before Samuel passed through their hunting grounds.[7] John Rogers remembered that he had never seen so many horses at one and the same time as these Indians had rounded up, but his father reports no trouble as he and his family settled down for the last four weeks of their long journey.

The previous four months of ever-increasing fatigue had taxed everyone's patience, resilience, and physical strength to the utmost. Constant vigilance by day and guard duties by night were taking their toll. Though there had been no loss of life, and scarcely any sickness of note, all were close to exhaustion. Their power to overcome the unknown dangers of each day was almost gone. John Rogers often wondered how his mother—tiny in build—managed to survive so many arduous camp duties with no experience of roughing it, accustomed as she was to being waited on by servants both in Cornwall and Wisconsin. Only through a spirit of co-operation, a sense of community and an unshakeable belief in God's protective mercy was it possible for them to outlive their ordeals. A feeling of isolation and of losing the battle against the might of nature was a common enemy because the Oregon Trail, as with the California Trail, was a one-way highway. Other wagons might overtake you and welcoming voices might ask to join you—but there was never the cloud of dust on the ever-retreating horizon that heralded an eastbound traveller who could tell you what pitfalls lay head. The constant enemies were the punishing dust kicked up by lumbering oxen, the everlasting glare of the sun, hot whining winds, the mysterious headaches, the perpetual anxiety about water and fuel, mountain sickness and valley fever, and aching wear and tear of rocks and stones on feet, hooves and the tyres of wheels. The humans became dehydrated and so did the wheels that carried them: the emigrants vomited, wood shrank and spokes fell by the wayside, causing delays and exasperation. Fortunately farmer Samuel was a genius at improvisation and had mastered all the basic skills for survival.

The final effort of Samuel's party began on 11 August with a struggle of 28 miles through sterile and sandy country, the last 18 miles with no signs of water, until the wagons halted at the Umatilla trading post of the Hudson's Bay Company. The following day they reached the Umatilla River and its 'plenty of grass', and on the 13th sighted the Columbia River, the great waterway that would guide them to the Pacific Ocean itself. But the struggle was far from over because before them straddled the volcanic Cascade Mountains, notorious for their bogs of mud. 'All the way very heavy travelling over sand hills', murmured Samuel, and that was not all. They were now following the western course of the Columbia, not along its banks, but along the top of a high bluff, from which they were obliged to descend steep slopes in order to cross unexpected and often hidden tributaries. On 15 August, relates Samuel, they descended 'a bad road, rocky and sandy', to Willow Creek, and again two days later over 'dreadful hills' to ford the John Day River in its sunken valley. This in itself was not too difficult a feat, though Samuel described it as a 'bad rocky stream' which so exhausted them they had to rest a night at Spanish Hollow on a bar of the Columbia River. But sleep was denied them. John Rogers summed up the feelings of all: 'The strong westerly wind on the mighty Columbia made sleeping under old quilts anything but desirable'. They huddled against each other for warmth but he found little comfort because 'I slept between brother Samuel and father and I thought their clothing smelt strong. I found a big body louse crawling on my shirt.'

Above the John Day River towered peaks of immaculate beauty and the valley was so immense it seemed to dwarf people, wagons and cattle into insignificance. Yet onwards they pressed, on 20 August gaining the mouth of the Deschutes River where it empties itself into the Columbia. Here was a ferry at a price of five dollars a wagon. Indians were hired to drive the cattle across by the old ruse of hanging on to their tails, the reluctant oxen then struggling to reach the opposite bank as soon as possible to get rid of the Indians. This crossing was usually regarded as dangerous on account of striking bargains with the Indians, but Samuel seems to have experienced no trouble. Only 15 miles away lay The Dalles and the Columbia River where they knew transportation to Portland was available. So, while the wagon train rested at Five Mile Creek, Samuel rode ahead to The Dalles to make arrangements. On his return they hitched the oxen and almost sauntered to the river for they now knew for certain that the end of their journey was almost in sight. As they climbed the hill between Five Mile Creek and The Dalles John Rogers and his brothers met two horsemen. Not only only were they driving oxen that were fat, but they also looked well-fed themselves and were actually wearing 'store clothing' and not homespun. They were on their way to greet relatives and friends from the east further back on the trail. One of the men, looking the boys over as they passed, was heard to remark: 'I looked just like that when I came over the trail years ago.' For the first time in many months the Cornish boys became sensitive about their personal appearance. They wore only 'portions' of a pair of cotton pants, no hat or shoes, and their hair was tangled and matted. The older boys, Samuel and William, were bearded. John Rogers felt a slow movement along the top of his head and brushed off a caterpillar with the remark: 'I guess he was trying to make a nest there.'[8]

At The Dalles Samuel decided to part company with his books so that their passage overland through the dreaded Cascades would be easier. They were shipped to Portland on an ancient sailing ship, *The Louisiana*, that plied for trade along the Columbia River. The total cost was 20 dollars. The boys and the oxen perhaps shed no tears to see the last of this heavy load of learning and culture, though in later years John Rogers regretted that he and his brothers never found time to read their parent's books because 'with us on the frontier there was always so much doing either of hard work or active play that we used up all our energies on these things'. Was this a clear case of *qui s'excuse s'accuse?*

The last 130 miles overland from The Dalles would have been too great a trial for the weakened oxen, as events were to show. In earlier days the Oregon Trail had terminated at The Dalles, which became known as The Landing. But the river route from there to Portland was notorious because it was costly and dangerous. The wheels were removed and the wagons floated down river and through the rapids, where many an emigrant was drowned and a cargo lost. In 1845 Samuel Kimbrough Barlow, who was in a party of 66 wagons led by one Solomon Tethrow, determined to find a safer route by land round Mt Hood, which later became variously known as the Barlow Road, the Barlow Trail and the Barlow Cut-off.[9] Of invaluable help in the subsequent development of Oregon Territory, it was a straight, almost Roman, up-and-down road leading southwards to Tygh Valley and then westwards to the Cascades pass which Samuel calls Barlow's Gate, but south of the 11,245 foot Mount Hood, named in 1792 after the British Admiral. The road ran through some of the most beautiful mountain scenery in the world, with ponderosa pine, small oaks, manzanita and incense, but Samuel had little time to admire them. 'Dreadful hills to go down and up over', he lamented at the end of a gruelling 16-mile day on 24 August.

It was south of Mount Hood that the party 'floundered in Oregon mud', the like of which they had never encountered before, not even in Cornwall. John Rogers told his father of an old Oregon pioneer in Iowa who had warned them: 'And you are going to Oregon? I've been there. You will climb Vinegar Hill and wade through powerful muck before you get there.' Samuel described the road as being 'rough with rocks, roots and stumps—a horrible mud hole'. Some wagons bounced over beds of roots, overturned, and then collapsed with broken wheels and shafts, so that a whole day was needed for repairs. Clothing became caked with mud as feet and legs tried to find a firm bottom away from the innumerable pits of mud. John Rogers actually saw one disconsolate traveller trying to extract from a mud-hole a bed-roll containing a feather bed. Moody and despairing, they thought this volcanic waste around Mount Hood really was the world's end, a 'weird place' where steam gushed and hissed from vents in the mountain's side, and bubbles burst and plopped with a disgusting sound from swamps of mud, so that it was impossible to find one sweet blade of grass for the cattle.

The oxen stumbled into more troubles on 29 August when they began tackling Laurel Hill, wrongly named by the early pioneers who thought the wild rhododendrons to be laurel. A broken ridge about four miles long, it was generally reckoned to provide the thickest and vilest mud in 2,000 miles, a place to be dreaded, and the most difficult of all the hills on the trail because neither beast nor humans could ever find a firm footing. In his bewilderment Samuel simply described it as a 'tremendous mud hole' and 'one of the worst in the world' for its ascent demanded eight yoke of oxen to drag a single wagon through the squelching mud. The descent was highly dangerous too. The wagons simply slid down the slope as if they were on ice, trees fastened to the rear wheels to act as brakes.

Two more trials of strength, endurance and patience awaited them. First there was the crossing of the Sandy River, which had to be made six times. Then, on 1 September, John Rogers's eleventh birthday, they made the last difficult climb, over the Devil's Backbone in drizzling rain through dense forest and over the roughest ground. The boy was not at all happy. From the summit of the Cascades he looked westwards to the heavy clouds of mists swirling and rolling through the Willamette valley, their 'long looked for destination', and was sad: 'I felt a little bit lonesome. We were leaving the broad dry plains and warm sand underfoot, the clear skies overhead with warm starlight nights.' There were more hard tasks to finish, the immediate one that of preparing the wagons for the descent from the Devil's Backbone. The oxen were unyoked and the wagons eased down the slopes by ropes wound round trees, while the cattle were left to slide down on their haunches as best they could.

But that was the last of their real trials. 'Bad hills' still dominated their landscape, extracting the last ounce of muscle from tired and blistered limbs, but on 3 September they came upon 'the first sight of civilisation', the trading post owned by Philip Foster (1805–1884), the pioneer who built the toll road with Sam Barlow. Emigrants were usually invited to help themselves, having run out of ready cash, but Samuel seems to have had enough money to buy his family their first potatoes, turnips and fresh cabbage. It was raining hard as they moved on a few miles from Foster's Place, as it was popularly called, amongst a profusion of wild fruits, Oregon grapes and ripening huckleberries, but they were still far from any place they could call home. Suddenly they saw a cabin in a wood. The door was wide open, they called but there was no answer, and they saw a large fireplace. Tired and wet, they could not resist the temptation to enter, build a fire and turn the cattle loose to forage. As dusk fell, a tall man with a rifle over his shoulder entered and seemed not at all surprised to see these strangers making themselves at home. Such hospitality was taken for granted on the moving frontier. The name of the owner of the cabin was Richardson. He had been deer hunting, but in his spare time was a potter.

From Richardson's cabin the travellers pressed on westward, endured a rough crossing of the Clackamas River, rested for three days, and on 9 September reached Milwaukie on the Willamette River. It was a small saw-mill town with a harbour, where they were excited to see sailing vessels being loaded with timber for San Francisco. To these Cornish folk it must have seemed that their wheel had now come full circle. From the Lizard Peninsula, washed by the waters of the English Channel, they had risked the gales and high seas of the Atlantic to reach Wisconsin and now, after crossing a land mass of 2,453 miles and almost entirely on foot, they stood within sight and earshot of the Pacific. On their first evening in Milwaukie, which must have reminded them so forcibly of many harbours in Cornwall, notably Porthleven and Penzance, Samuel read the 23rd Psalm to his gathered family and friends, then fell upon his knees and thanked God for all His goodness shown to his family on their long journey. He could surely afford to congratulate himself too for, through his wisdom, prudence and skilful planning and management, not one person had been lost or been seriously ill. Even the scholarship of the Old World had been enabled to make a successful transfer to the New World. The links between labour and learning, between the hand that could mend a wagon wheel and shoe an ox and the hand that could fashion an apt phrase in his journal, were so strong that no disaster could break them. On the contrary, they could make a sea and land change, at once rich and rare, out of which emerged the new Americans to whom these Cornish now belonged.

NOTES

1. Samuel James's Journal, entry for 14 July 1851.
2. Autobiography of John Rogers James (1916).
3. Aubrey L. Haines, *Historic Sites along the Oregon Trail* (St Louis, 1983), pp. 326–9.
4. Fort Boise was a trading post of the Hudson's Bay Company on the east bank of the Snake River. It was severely damaged by flooding in 1853 and was not reoccupied (Haines, pp. 339–41).
5. Autobiography of John Rogers James (1916).
6. Ibid.
7. The Whitman massacre of 13 adults and two children together with the capture of more than 50 hostages and the burning of the mission building is a turning point in the history of Oregon. Joe Meek, a mountain-man, rode over the mountains in the dead of winter and reported the massacre to Washington D.C. in March 1848. Congress immediately granted territorial status to Oregon (Gregory M. Franzwa, *The Oregon Trail Revisited*, pp. 354–61). See also Erwin N. Thompson, *Whitman Mission*; National Historic Site (Washington, D.C., Government Printing Office), 92 pp. and Marvin M. Richardson, *The Whitman Mission: The Third Station on the Oregon Trail* (Walla Walla, Washington, 1940), 160 pp.
8. Autobiography of John Rogers James (1916).
9. For further information about the Barlow Road, see *Barlow Road 1845–6* (Wasco and Clackamas County Historical Societies, Portland, Oregon, 1975) and Mary S. Barlow, 'History of the Barlow Road' (*Oregon Historical Quarterly*, Vol. 3, March 1902), pp. 71–81.

CHAPTER 9

First Year in Oregon

Samuel James had reached the Oregon of his dreams. The banks of the River Clackamas, fringed with willow and vine maple, coursed through sloping prairie lands that beckoned the plough. Land was here for the asking and Samuel was ready to ask. He must have been bone-weary, physically and mentally exhausted, after bringing his family safely over raw trails that defied and defeated thousands, decimated families and left untold numbers of dead in hastily-marked graves in the deserts and mountains. And if Samuel was frayed to a frazzle, one can wonder at the weariness of Anna Maria, the small, tough-minded, brown-eyed girl he had married in St Keverne. She had willingly and devotedly followed Samuel from the comforts of Trelan across the perilous Atlantic to Wisconsin swamplands, then over plains and deserts and unmapped mountains to an Oregon Country peopled by scattered whites and apprehensive red men. Her reaction was one of acceptance, of faith and even enthusiasm.

Anna Maria was now 46, her husband a year older. Their Cornish-born sons were maturing into manhood. Young Samuel was now 17, stout and dependable; William, at 15, was an able teamster; Thomas, 13, could ride and shoot, and Johnny, who lived to tell so much of this family saga, was a nimble 10-year-old, wide-eyed at the spectacle he was watching. The younger children, all born in Wisconsin, were headed by Eliza, a responsible eight-year-old who worked at her mother's elbow, helping to care for and comfort the little ones, Richard Oregon, now five, and the three-year-old twins, Mary Ann Frances and her brother, Allen.

Samuel's prayers at the safe deliverance of his family in Oregon echoed the feelings of his wife. Theirs was a team bonded in faith and devotion. Both recognised the years of struggle they faced in settling on land, building a new home in a strange and wild environment and winning new friends in the westernmost outpost of the America they had chosen. These first days in Oregon revealed little of the privations and turmoil the coming months would bring. A foothold on the Clackamas, near present Milwaukie and but eight miles from

Portland, now Oregon's greatest city, offered Samuel the immediate starting point he sought. Others in his little wagon train, notably the Daniel Lucas family, rolled their wagons southward into central Oregon. Samuel rented land and a cabin. Winter was coming and he was intent on securing his family and animals in an untested climate, planning ahead to the setting out of orchards and crops in the Spring. Anna Maria soon converted the interior of her crude cabin into a make-do home. Her cows were generous with milk and there was a market for butter in Milwaukie village. John Rogers recalled his first experience at peddling his mother's butter. When the storekeeper asked if the butter was fresh, young John had responded 'No' and was given the butter to take home. 'Why Johnny, you saw me make it only yesterday', said Anna Maria. 'Yes, but I saw you put salt in it', Johnny responded.

During the winter of 1851–52, a season light in snow but dampened by weeks of a drizzle he came to know as 'Oregon mist', Samuel bought additional acreage and built a cabin large enough for his family of ten. He and his older sons cleared land, installed rail fences and set out apple, pear and plum trees. Here Anna Maria found everything necessary to make the homestead comfortable and even delightful for, as she says, a clear brook ran singing along within a few yards of the door, and they were surrounded by the grandest mountain scenery.[1]

This first farm on the Clackamas did not turn out to be the paradise Samuel had anticipated. The pasturage for his cattle proved unsuitable and they wandered on to neighbours' properties to graze. Springtime also brought the family down with chills and fevers too much like those they had endured in Wisconsin for seven years. Sons Samuel and William were old enough to press their own opinions. They wanted to explore the areas south and north of Milwaukie. Father Samuel listened and agreed the vast territory offered other possibilities. Daniel Lucas found grass as high as his knees in February at the headwaters of the Willamette. Passing travellers claimed that even better prospects existed at Puget Sound. Each month brought reports of new settlements. It made sense to Samuel that if their Milwaukie location was inferior, the time to move their wagons was immediately, before their roots were too deep and before the continuing stream of westbound settlers overran lands which could be theirs. Moving either south down the Willamette Valley or across the Columbia River into Puget Sound country 100 miles north offered much more favourable conditions than the family had encountered on the Oregon Trail. Travel in either direction would be in valleys rather than across hulking hills and mountains. Massive forests blanketing western Oregon contained prairie openings, treeless and waving in deep bunch grass. Water was abundant and Indians at this time were accepting the presence of white newcomers.

Thus it was decided in the Spring of 1852 that Samuel and his son, William, aged 16, would go north toward the Puget Sound country which the British explorer, Captain George Vancouver, had charted 60 years earlier. After the first grain crop at Milwaukie was harvested in late summer, father Samuel and son

William in August set out afoot to find a new location. They were gone a month, disappearing into a wilderness of Douglas fir forests which some day would become one of America's greatest sources of timber for domestic and foreign buyers. Their journey with Indian boatmen took them down the Willamette River from Milwaukie into the great Columbia and northward to the mouth of a smaller river, the Cowlitz. Up that stream lay Cowlitz Landing, a point from which travellers afoot and on horseback commenced their land journey into what is now the State of Washington. Samuel and his son were the first emigrants from Cornwall to set foot on that land.[2]

Seventy miles north of the Cowlitz, Samuel and William emerged from dark forests into open prairie. They looked for miles across level land carpeted with hip-high grass. Near the centre of this prairie rose a mound with a commanding view of the entire prairie. Samuel James had arrived at Grand Mound. Other white men had crossed this prairie. The Scottish botanist, David Douglas, after whom the fir tree is named, had seen it in 1827. The American explorer, Capt. Charles Wilkes, had noted its 'park-like beauty' in his 1841 expedition.[3] Other wagon-train pioneers had crossed Grand Mound prairie in earlier years but their eyes were on the waterfront and timberlands of Puget Sound, 20 miles north. Samuel was the first to see Grand Mound Prairie as a new homeland, a farm site he could develop without fighting giant trees, a land open to the plough and to fencing into pastures. He chose lands between the Chehalis River and a meandering stream he called Scatter Creek.

Samuel and William, weary but pleased with their discoveries, returned to Milwaukie in September. Anna Maria knew by the look in Samuel's eyes that he had found a better spot. After warm greetings and embraces, Samuel told of the new country he had found, the 'home in the West' that had been his magnet of withdrawal from Wisconsin. Anna Maria saw the fires of new adventure in his eyes. Ever trusting and supportive, she agreed to pulling up stakes immediately and moving on to Grand Mound. 'There someday', she told John Rogers, 'the butter market will be even better than in Milwaukie.' He recalled the events of the autumn of 1852:[4]

> You can imagine the excitement. We were seasoned travellers but this was a move which would test the bravest; we located only eight miles from Portland and there were settlements all around us; Lewellin with his nursery of which Father was so fond, was right at hand, stately ships came and went on the Willamette River. We were now to leave all this and make our settlement in a part of Oregon Territory where . . . our nearest white neighbour would be six miles away and where we would be literally surrounded by the native Indians.

Again the creaky wagons which had swayed and bounced across deserts and mountains were loaded with family possessions, including the books. Of all things watched by Samuel James as his wife and sons packed away the furnishings we can be assured he eyed most intently the safe storage of his library.

It was the good fortune of the Jameses to make their move northward in a year when Dr John McLoughlin was the head of the Hudson's Bay Company in Oregon. A factor of great character and kindness to American citizens coming into English-claimed territory, McLoughlin approved Samuel's request to purchase an old Hudson's Bay trading craft, a bateau, which Samuel and his sons repaired. As John Rogers recorded:

> We loaded our knocked-down wagons, chains, yokes and household goods into the clumsy but manageable old craft and with four oars and the assistance of two gentlemen passengers who wanted to work their way to Puget Sound, we made our way down the Willamette into the mighty Columbia River. Father had hired some Indians and how they would sing as they paddled the boat 12 miles downstream to the Columbia, along that river eastward for forty miles and then up the smaller but very swift Cowlitz River. Here is where the Indian is seen at his best, pulling and paddling a boat up the swift current of a forceful stream. With steady stroke and keen eye for hazards, he missed nothing.

In fact the Cowlitz, 'a beautiful stream' to Anna Maria, was so swift that only the Indians could navigate it.

The Cornish family, their two travellers and the Indian boatmen camped overnight at a place called Coffin Rock, an ancient Indian burial ground which in modern years was torn away by developers hungering for cheap building stone. John Rogers remembers the piercing look and firm answer Anna Maria gave a ship's captain and his wife who came from a lumber-hauling vessel docked at Coffin Rock. 'They explained they had no children and wanted Mother to give them our sister, eight-year-old Eliza, whose bright eyes and rosy cheeks fascinated them. Mother firmly told them civilised parents don't give away their children.' At another camping place on the Cowlitz River, little Mary Ann and Allen, the four-year-old twins, were desolate over the loss of the rooster and hen they were bringing as their possessions from Milwaukie. After much searching, the Indians found the rooster perched high in a tree and they managed to wave it down to rejoin the children. But the hen was gone for good and the Indians gave their opinion it had been eaten by a 'tenas puss-puss', a little panther.

The distance between Grand Mound and the Cowlitz Landing where boats brought travellers moving northward is less than 60 miles. It can be spanned by automobile today in about one hour. Paved highways now ribbon through a countryside once thickset with Douglas fir trees of great diameter. In the time of the Jameses the journey took 12 to 15 days, a staggering trek around fallen trees, clutching vines and brambles, through mud and sinuous creeks. Aware of what lay ahead through the advice of John R. Jackson, a warm-hearted Englishman whose home is still preserved as the 'Jackson courthouse', Samuel James and family waited two weeks for the cattle which sons Samuel and William were driving over difficult trails after swimming their animals across the

Columbia, Lewis and Cowlitz rivers. 'When they reached us, their clothes were in rags and they were almost barefooted', wrote John Rogers. 'Samuel had an old boot tied on one foot and a ragged shoe on the other.'

Together again, the family once more loaded its wagons, hitched the oxen, and were on their way to a new home at Grand Mound. Samuel James had selected 320 acres which for a few years after 1851 the United States government granted free to citizens coming into this part of Oregon. Upon this land a small log cabin without a door or windows had been built by a trapper known as Tenas Jack (Little John) and abandoned by him when newly discovered gold beckoned to him from California.[5] It was something to shelter the family against winter rains which were in season when the Jameses moved toward Grand Mound. In later years, the youngest daughter, Mary Ann Frances, recalled that final day of travel:

> Mother looked very happy sitting on a roll of bedding with her knitting. I do not remember how many days we were on the road but I do remember some of the awful mudholes where the men had to put their shoulders to the sides of the wagons to keep from overturning. I recall camping one evening along the banks of the Chehalis River at the Joe Borst farm. We children saw him, a bachelor, paring potatoes. We saw him throw peelings on the ground and we ran and picked them up, begging Mother to cook them for us. Poor little wretches, Borst exclaimed and then brought Mother a generous pan of potatoes.

About mid-day on 12 October 1852, the James 'wagon train' came out of the forest onto the level floor of Grand Mound prairie. Mary Ann never forgot that day:[6]

> As we passed by the Mound a soft-footed coyote came running down the side of the hillock and trotted behind the wagon. We children, seated in the back of the wagon, called out to Mother to see the pretty dog trailing after us. Mother told me years after that this was the first time a great fear came over her, when she realised she and Samuel had brought their family into a wild country where not even the wild animals were afraid of us. Brother Samuel was driving our wagon. We soon reached the little cabin where Father and the boys were waiting for us. Father was talking to a stranger, whose family, we soon found, occupied the cabin. Indians, in swarms, surrounded all, and I was terribly frightened. The strange man was a Mr Rutledge, who had arrived a few days before us from Portland. Father was explaining that he had placed a claim on the cabin a month earlier and had returned to Milwaukie to bring us all north.
>
> So we were left peaceably in possession. Father found a big cedar log which he sawed in proper length for a door and neatly split a plank six feet long and three feet wide. It could not be put up that night so Mother hung up a quilt before the open door. Along in the evening this was pushed aside. Mother, thinking it an Indian, pushed the quilt still farther back, and there stood a great grey wolf. Mother really shrieked and the wolf fled. A few nights after, it killed a little calf and it in turn was killed by Father putting strychnine in the calf's body. In the mean time the door was hung by leather hinges cut from Brother Samuel's old boot.

The Jameses were in their new home, such as it was.

NOTES

1. Anna Maria to her sister Elizabeth Foxwell Shephard in Yorkville, Wisconsin, 14 November 1852. See also David James, *From Grand Mound to Scatter Creek*, p. 23.
2. David James, p. 26.
3. Ray Allen Billington, *Westward Expansion*, p. 523.
4. Autobiography of John Rogers James (1916).
5. David James, p. 26.
6. Journal of Mary Ann Frances James Shephard (1911).

Mound Prairie Chehalis River, nea
Wm Ford's Tavern Lewis County Oreg
Territory 14 Novr 1852

y dear Elizabeth

I believe this is the first letter I have addressed to
ou since we removed from Wisconsin and I feel truly thankful to s
that through the infinite mercy of God both my family and self hav
en in the enjoyment of excellent uninterrupted health. The last letter w
ceived from Wisconsin was from my brother Thomas complaining of o
ng silence we found so that the James' long letter containing an account
ur [illegible] arrival in Oregon — our having made a claim on the Plain
[illegible] with a description of it — and all our progress up to Februa
st. [illegible] begineth the next chapter. About the middle of Marc
e removed into our new log house here we found every thing nece
make a homestead comfortable and even delightful a beautiful bu
[illegible] spot on a pleasant knoll of considerable extent — a clear brook ran
[illegible] along within a few yards of our door and surrounded by the g
t mountain scenery — and more than all decidedly healthy — a
walking distance of Oregon city and Milwaukie and eight miles of
th all these advantages the boys could not reconcile themselves to it on acc
the great lack of grass which prevailed [illegible] prevailed for twenty miles —
wth of all description Hazel Raspberry, salal, Rose, Willow and fern grow to a
ost gigantic size and in February what appeared to us and others to be a [illegible]
grass spring up thickly over the ground and mountain sides nor was it till the [illegible]
n blossomed out that we discovered what we hoped would have been nouris
[illegible] for our cattle was nothing more than the geranium or grass [illegible]
nd fully accounted for the straying of our cattle and the constant hunt that
as kept up by our neighbours and selves after cattle and horses. In fac
e now found that this was no place for cattle till it had been subdued a
ut into cultivation — to make the matter worse we were every now and the
n the receipt of messages and accounts from our friends and acquaintances
[illegible] located, some in the Umpqua, some in the Willamette Valley — some

CHAPTER 10

Starting Anew at Grand Mound

What Grand Mound prairie offered as a new homesite was described by Anna Maria James in a letter to her sister, Elizabeth Foxwell Shephard, living in Yorkville, Wisconsin, dated 14 November 1852.[1] 'I believe this is the first letter I have addressed to you since my removal from Wisconsin and I feel truly thankful to say that through the infinite mercy of God both my family and self have been in the enjoyment of excellent uninterrupted health,' she wrote. 'So, here beginneth the next chapter.'

Conserving her limited supply of writing paper, Anna Maria deliberately spaced the lettering and lines of her letter so that she could write first crosswise until the page was filled, then turn it to write lengthwise with equal legibility:

> Many and many a year have passed since I have enjoyed life as I have since I have been in Oregon . . . The Chehalis River is one of the most beautiful in Oregon. Our claim stretches a mile along the banks of it. The river flows through an elevated part of the country and our house, within a few rods of the river, has one of the finest views in Oregon. The prairies stretching away to the north like a fine lawn are skirted on each side by oaks and maples at this time in all the brilliant hues of autumn. Behind, on gently rising hills, are forests of fir and cedar of the most gigantic height and size. Farther still to the northeast rises the ever-snowclad Mt Rainier and southward can be seen the magnificent cone of Mt St Helens.
>
> On the opposite side to the southwest is the Coast Range, so near that we can see the trees on them, so magnificent are those immense snowy mountains that none but those who have seen them can form any idea of them. This prairie takes its name from a remarkable mound about a mile from our house. It stands on about 25 acres and is 100 feet high with a fine spring half way up. The rest of this prairie, which is 10 miles long and from two to four miles in width, stretches away to the north of us and is watered with a beautiful stream called Scatter Creek. The prairie is covered with grass at this time as green as in May.

Opposite: *Part of a letter from Anna Maria James, Grand Mound, Oregon, 14 November 1852, to her sister Elizabeth in Wisconsin.* Photograph, slightly reduced in size, by courtesy of David James

> The soil of the Mound has just enough clay to make it rich and excellent. The rest of the prairie is deficient of clay. It has a rich black mould averaging two feet deep resting on a substrata of sand and gravel which in some places is so mixed with the soil as to give it the name of a gravel prairie. You might have the choice of 50 such prairies as this and some better on the river. Farmers were never better paid in the world. I now milk three cows. We have four and Mr James means to have two more and a few sheep. Mr James sold the worst yoke of cattle he had the other day for $160.

Anna Maria mentioned she had been churning butter and now had on hand 26 pounds which would bring her 60 to 70 cents per pound. Their only near neighbours were native Indians.

> We are the only inhabitants of this great prairie except for a few Indians who have a fishing station about a mile from us. These are on very friendly terms with us, supplying us with venison, wild fowl and floor mats (woven from cedar bark) at a very reasonable price and we in turn letting them have what flour and molasses we can at a reasonable price which they are always willing to pay, bartering what they had for what we had. Soap is another article I am glad to see in request among them and it affords them no little amusement to look at the engraving plates in the Encyclopedia, which Father and the older boys often open to show them pictures of animals and events far beyond their world. They are the stoutest and finest set of Indians we have seen. We converse with them by means of a jargon composed of English, French and Chinook, which the Indians speak and we are glad to 'waw waw' (speak) pretty well.
>
> My children I am thankful to say look better than I ever saw them in Eastern America. They have not had the least symptom of any of the diseases, from the fever and ague to the sorehead, that they were so afflicted with in Wisconsin. It makes me very sad to think how we are separated as a family, never to meet again (at least in all probability) under one roof. Oh that we may all meet at last at the right hand of God. Let this be our sole concern. You have the advantage of us in schools, churches and society but I feel quite patient to await the arrival of those blessings in addition to those that we enjoy.
>
> Now I suppose I must look on all this as a Utopian dream as I expect few if any of you would barter your comfortable home for a log cabin. Well, it is my home and I hope I have not given an exaggerated description of it. I often thought last year that we had bettered our condition from what we were in Wisconsin and now I think we have ours ten times beyond what we were then.

And her letter closed with, 'All the children send their kindest love to you all. I feel thankful for a few flower seeds.'

The new homeland of Samuel James was a gravel prairie and a rippling river which the Scottish botanist, David Douglas, after his seed-seeking forays into the Pacific Northwest in 1826–27, described as 'a stream nearly as large as the Thames, very rapid with numerous cascades'. Grand Mound prairie and the Chehalis flowing into Grays Harbor were to be the arenas in which the Cornish farmer performed his duties, cast his views and notched his place in Washington Territorial history during the final 14 years of his life.

The quick-moving Chehalis challenged all who wrestled with its riffles (choppy water), its meandering nature, its floods and shallows. It is a long river twisting some 125 miles from sources in slopes of Washington's greatest mountain, Rainier, 14,410 feet, to the sandbars rimming Grays Harbor where it smashes headlong into the Pacific Ocean. Running east to west, the Chehalis is the greatest drainage for tributary streams between the Fraser River in British Columbia and the mighty Columbia River which forms the boundary between the states of Washington and Oregon. Indians called 'Chehalis' have populated the river into ages beyond reach. (The word 'Chehalis' is a place-name meaning 'sandy region'.) They were first seen by white men who ventured across the American continent before the Colonies rebelled. The first seafaring explorer to confront their canoes was the Yankee fur trader, Captain Robert Gray, out of Boston, who brought his ship, *Columbia*, across the treacherous bar on 7 May 1792. His reward from history was the naming of Grays Harbor in his honour. Mounting ten guns, the *Columbia* overwhelmed the natives who paddled and babbled around her after Gray dropped anchor. Gray was after otter skins for the China trade. He made good deals for his investors. In one transaction with Indians north of Grays Harbor he obtained 200 sea otter pelts worth $8,000 in exchange for one old iron chisel worth just about nothing. As trading stock, Gray carried beads, brass buttons, earrings, calico, tin mirrors, hatchets, copper kettles, snuff, tobacco, iron bars, nails and other hardware exciting to people called savages.

Gray brought the natives not only baubles but their first smell of gunpowder and pain of grapeshot. Gray's official log of his debut in the harbour mentions trading but no difficulties other than shallow sandbars. Fortunately for history, John Boit, Jr, age 16, was aboard as fifth mate. In his journals[2] he reported that the Indians were so persistent in approaching the *Columbia* to trade and look and feel (and steal) that late one night their presence in numbers deemed threatening by the captain resulted in orders to touch off the cannon. Boit said the *Columbia* was on the north side of the harbour. This placed the ship within sight of an offshore reddish stone pillar later to become a memorial to Samuel James, known as 'James Rock'.

Boit put these comments about conflict with the Indians into his diary:

> Vast many canoes came off, full of Indians. They appear'd to be a savage set, and was well arm'd, every man having his Quiver and Bow slung over his shoulder. Without doubt we are the first civilised people that ever visited this port, and these poor fellows view'd us and the Ship with great astonishment. Their language was different from any we had yet heard. The men were entirely naked, and the women, except for a small apron before made of rushes, were also in a state of nature. They was stout made, and very ugly. Their canoes was from the logs rudely cut out, with upright ends. We purchas'd many furs and fish. . . .
>
> This evening heard the hooting of the Indians, and all hands was immediately under arms. Several canoes was seen passing near the Ship, but was dispersed by firing a few muskets over their heads. At midnight we heard them again, and soon

> after, as it was bright moonlight, we saw the Canoes approaching the Ship. We fired several cannon over them, but they still persisted to advance, with the war Hoop. At length a large canoe with at least 20 men in her got within 1/2 pistol shot of the quarter, and with a Nine pounder, loaded with Buck shot, we dash'd her all to pieces and no doubt kill'd every soul in her. The rest soon made a retreat. I do not think they had any conception of the power of Artillery.

The very next day, 9 May 1792, the Indians came back with others from down river, not to attack again but to point out the wondrous and terrible thing that had happened the previous night. They were there to trade again.

> I am sorry we was obliged to kill the poor Divells but it cou'd not with safety be avoided. These natives brought us some fine Salmon, and plenty of Beaver skins, with some Otters, and I believe had we staid longer among them we shou'd have done well.

In his history of Grays Harbor, Edwin Van Syckle[3] wrote 'Geologic digs in recent decades reveal that Indians were on the Coast hundreds of years before the first white men came to "discover" what the Indians had discovered centuries before.'

> They had a sophisticated culture and art of high order. They could snare salmon, hunt seal and whale, weave bark and reed fabrics, cure meat and other foods. The Chehalis Indians, like all fellow tribes on the Northwest coast, travelled the lengths of their rivers and ventured out into the Pacific Ocean in beautifully fashioned canoes hollowed from enormous cedar trees which they shaped with fire and scraped with antlers and stones.

When the first whites appeared as trappers and explorers early in the nineteenth century there were perhaps no more than 1,000 native inhabitants in the entire Chehalis Valley stretching west from Grand Mound prairie 60 miles to the sea. Unlike tent-dwelling Indians who lived in skin-covered tepees east of the Cascade Mountains which divide Washington into two quite different climates, wet and dry, the Chehalis built their houses with split cedar boards. The Wilkes Exploring Expedition of 1841 (only a decade ahead of Samuel James) found the Chehalis Indians well supplied with blankets, muskets and knives. Captain Charles Wilkes's exploring party reported:

> They are excessively fond of tabacco and invariably swallow the smoke, and often times retain it so long in the stomach as to throw into convulsions. They enjoy a high reputation as warriors, for which reason they are much dreaded by their neighbours who are of a more peaceful character.

The Chehalis tribe had long engaged in trading with the fierce and powerful Makahs who inhabited the upper Olympic Peninsula. The Makahs had traded with Captain George Vancouver, the English explorer, who gave them muskets, lead balls and powder for their beaver pelts. In turn, the Makahs had passed these 'sticks that roar' along to the Chehalis.

Slavery was practised among the more powerful Indians who preyed upon their weaker neighbours and sometimes raided each other in their quest for additional women and male 'servants'. Communication between the diverse regional tribes was done through a trade language which the whites termed 'Chinook jargon'. Van Syckle observed that the jargon had probably existed for centuries as a purely Indian creation before whites realised that the natives were using two languages, their own tribal dialects and a second language familiar to all tribes. As versatile with words as they were proficient with nature's physical offerings, the Indians quickly incorporated English and French words into their language. Water, for instance, in their jargon was called 'chuck'. Indians knew salt and valued it highly. When they heard whites talk about salt, they knew that was the flavour of ocean water, which they then began calling 'salt chuck', a term used to this day.

Chehalis Indians usually formed small villages of a few families at favourable fishing, hunting and berry picking locations along the river. One such village stood near the Mound in 1852. John Rogers wrote: 'An Indian village was on the bank of the Chehalis River where it washes right up to the prairie. Near the Mound and a half mile east of our cabin were two families, the Hatstute and the We-i-we families. We-i-we had a wife and three sons, Tesian, Colollowan and Heom.'[4]

Surely these Indians looked different to Anna Maria, raised as she was in a contrasting culture of formality and 'civilised customs', but it was the small James daughters, Eliza and Mary Ann, who wrinkled their noses at what confronted them. Anna Maria, in the manner of the lady she had learned to be, gave not a sign of noticing anything out of the ordinary. But Mary Ann observed bluntly:[5]

> When we unyoked our cattle on the land my Father had taken as a donation claim, we found ourselves among a lot of dirty, filthy, smelly Indians; not the kind we read in the Leather Stocking tales written so beautifully by James Fenimore Cooper. There was nothing romantic about them. I can remember climbing under one of the wagons to hide from them. The next morning after moving into our log cabin we were almost swamped by the Indians crowding in, some of the men quite naked. These Father sent away to put their blankets around them. The squaws were a little more modestly dressed—a short shirt and a skirt of bark strips about their loins.
>
> As time went on Mother was much concerned for fear we would pick up some of their peculiar habits. One of these was pushing their lips out as far as possible when talking to us. We children thought it very funny and, of course, tried to imitate them. Once, when a lot of Indian children were playing about our house, Mother said 'Why there's a little white boy!', and so he proved to be, belonging to our nearest neighbour five miles away. He had come with the Indian children with whom he was accustomed to play. It did not seem to have done him any harm as he afterwards became a prominent minister in San Francisco.

White men were no strangers to the Chehalis people by 1852 but the first white woman and the first white children they saw were Anna Maria James and her little tots. From that first confrontation between nude natives and clothed Cornishmen, Anna Maria spared no efforts to teach her new neighbours the Cornish versions of cleanliness, modesty, housekeeping and cooking. She instructed the wives of Hatstute and We-i-we in the use and making of soft soap, emphasising that cleanliness was next to Godliness. She found the squaws so interested in lathering their hands and bodies with 'white mud' that they were inclined to take it without asking until taught principles of respecting private property. Mary Ann remembered that 'Once an old squaw stole a silver spoon from us and traded it to one of our white neighbours for a gallon of soap. Mother, taking dinner at their house, spied her spoon and laid claim to it.'

The Indian women learned from Anna Maria how to sew cloth, knit and braid rag rugs. The men learned from Samuel the mysteries of planting potatoes and wheat. In return, the Indians showed the Jameses how to weave from cedar bark and grasses, how to select edible wild berries and plants, how to hunt wild game, how to row dugout canoes and how to snare the wily salmon which were the mainstay of their food supply. Animals along the river valley included black bear, deer, beaver, otter, muskrats, red fox, marten, mink, skunks and coyotes. Ducks and geese came seasonally and there were owls, crows, eagles, osprey, woodpeckers and many song birds.

Here then was a merging of people of unlike backgrounds in what to Eastern Americans was a vast wilderness inhabited by ignorant savages. No doubt these newly arrived whites seemed equally strange in their customs and ways to the Indians. That they, whites and reds, accepted each other without hostility, despite backgrounds five thousand miles apart—from Grand Mound to Cornwall's Lizard Peninsula—supported Samuel's belief in what could be achieved by fair dealing with people of all colours.

The Indians responded warmly to the music their new neighbours introduced. Young Samuel fascinated them with his fiddling of bouncy tunes learned around evening campfires along the Oregon Trail. Mary Ann said that her mother, 'though not a Patti or a Melba', loved to sing while she worked about the house. The Indians would listen attentively and then say 'Hiow sharty semba' which meant 'Mother sings a great deal'. They were also lovers of pictures. Mary Ann describes how the chief borrowed her father's *London Encyclopedia*, the three volumes of which contained an abundance of illustrations: buildings of London, flowers, the anatomy of the human body, the national uniforms of soldiers and sailors etc. But only one volume a time was borrowed:

> Each book was placed upon a clean 'oliwequic' [mat] and the leaves most carefully turned: not a child was allowed to touch the book . . . When the book was not in use it was tied up in a clean bandanna handkerchief and hung to one of the rafters. We found the Indians very friendly and kind hearted. They were never tired of listening to Bible stories, especially of the creation and the Flood, and we were surprised to find they possessed legends of both of these events.

An old chief of the tribe became seriously ill in that first winter. He knew he was dying and he begged Samuel James to recite the Lord's Prayer to him over and over again. He wanted Samuel to repeat it at his funeral, which Samuel did.

NOTES

1. David James, *From Grand Mound to Scatter Creek*, pp. 23–8.
2. Now in the archives of the Massachusetts Historical Society, Boston.
3. Edwin Van Syckle, *The River Pioneers, Early Days on Grays Harbor*, ed. David James (Pacific Search Press, Seattle, Washington, 1982), 433 pp.
4. Autobiography of John Rogers James (1916).
5. Journal of Mary Ann Frances James Shephard (1911).

CHAPTER 11

Strains and Stresses

That first Fall and Winter on Grand Mound prairie imposed burdensome trials on Samuel and his family. Death took their infant son, Allen, twin brother of Mary Ann, only a few months after they settled into the cabin of Tenas Jack.

Immediately after settling in October 1852, Samuel hitched his oxen to a plough and, with four strong sons to help, commenced breaking the black prairie soil and fencing his fields. By Spring newcomers were seen straggling across the prairie, working their way northward to claim acreage still open to them. These travellers noted how well the Cornish were getting along with improvements. Samuel obtained a steel burr grist mill from George Bush, who was the first black immigrant to settle on Puget Sound and lived in a forest opening still called Bush prairie. Bush had arrived in Oregon in 1845 but headed north of the Columbia River when he was denied land because his skin was the wrong colour. The grist mill was fastened to a post on the James cabin porch and it was a daily chore for the younger boys to grind meal for the next breakfast. The cabin was becoming an overnight stopping point for travellers riding or walking toward the new settlement of Olympia, 20 miles north. These visitors would step out of the cabin to watch the boys crank their little mill. They would smile contentedly and comment on how rapidly conveniences were coming into these distant outposts.

Samuel bought his first sheep, seven head at seven dollars each, from George Bush. John Rogers recalled a disaster which followed:

> We younger children were told to watch the sheep but we played and allowed them to stray off. They were not found until the next day and most of them had been killed by coyotes. I remember only one ewe coming home from over Scatter Creek. Afterwards, Father and Brother Samuel walked 25 miles to Nisqually and bought forty-one head to herd home from James McAllister. I had gathered up seven dollars and fifty cents and sent it along to buy one sheep.

The Winter of 1852–53 brought two feet of snow which stayed on the ground for a month. To keep the hungry cattle alive, Samuel and his sons cut tender tree branches for them to browse on. The family had come onto the prairie too late in the year to put aside winter hay.

One day two men came staggering and falling through deep snow toward the James cabin. They were muttering strangely, incoherently. 'Father faced them at the cabin door,' recalled John Rogers. 'He thought by their actions the men were drunk.' The taller of the two men, supporting his slumped companion, asked for accommodation. Samuel pondered and responded that the cabin was crowded and in poor shape to care for more people. 'Well, my dear sir' said the taller stranger, 'This man is perishing.'

> Father stepped out of the door and helped them into our warm room. They were Enoch Chapman and Dr J. H. Roundtree. They had walked and waded over 100 miles from the Columbia River to Grays Harbor and were making their way up the Chehalis River when they upset at the mouth of Black River. Wet and nearly frozen, they had managed to find the trail to our cabin. Dr Roundtree's feet were badly frostbitten and he was laid up in our cabin nearly all winter with Mother and Father attending to his needs.

After the snow melted and travel conditions improved, Samuel James and his oldest son, Samuel, left on a three day trip to Tumwater and Olympia for needed supplies. It was while they were away that the youngest son, Allen, five years old, took sick with a feverish croup and died a day later, despite all that his mother could do with the few remedies available to her. John Rogers wrote:

> No death occurring in the family ever distressed us more than this, as we had come together so far into the wilderness. I remember that Father for a long time after this would take up the Bible and read and conduct family worship as a consolation for our bereavement. Two Indian brothers, Tesian and Collolowan, dug the grave on a slope between three towering fir trees within sight of the cabin. They brought two wide cedar boards from the roof of their house to make the coffin. This, we learned, was their custom when a friend died. We made a lonely little procession to the grave. Father and Mother led the way, followed by Eliza, Richard and little Allen's twin sister, Mary Ann. We four older brothers carried the small coffin. Dr Roundtree hobbled out on crutches to be with us and several Indians came close to stand around the grave as Father read the burial service.

Thirteen years passed before another family member died.

The year 1853 surged with new challenges and demands on the family. A winter within the cramped space of Tenas Jack's cabin wore out the patience of parents and children alike. They needed a larger house. It was Samuel's good fortune that three young men named Armstrong, Cox and Strahill cut a trail early in 1853 from Grand Mound to a site on Cedar Creek ten miles west where they built a water-powered sawmill. Their plan was to saw Douglas fir into heavy planks and raft them down the Chehalis to Grays Harbor for shipment to the booming city of San Francisco 700 miles down coast in California. As soon as Armstrong got his saw whirling, Samuel sent sons Samuel, William and John Rogers with oxen and a wagon to bring back the lumber needed to erect a new house. By Fall the home was ready, two stories high and with six bedrooms for the family, even an extra room for the ever-increasing overnight travellers, three fireplaces and a large living room with double glass doors. The cedar shakes (tiles) which shingled the roofs were hand split by the James boys from trees which Indians helped them cut down and shape with a sharp blade called a frow.

Leonard Durgan, a nurseryman from the American Middle West, had come early in the year to locate his donation claim around the big Mound. That Spring Durgan and another newcomer, Augustus Gangloff, started a nursery of apple, pear and plum trees. They were a joyful sight to Samuel, the constant orchardist, who had set out fruit trees when he first arrived in Wisconsin from Cornwall, and again at Milwaukie, Oregon in 1851. Samuel soon had ten acres of fruit trees growing on his river bottom land at the foot of a low hill near his new home. The first apples were from crabapple trees, on which he grafted several varieties, Roman, Russet, Red June and Golden Sweets. The Jameses had brought grain, garden and flower seeds from their first Oregon location and obtained more from some of the older settlers, including George Bush, their black friend. But they also sent to Cornwall for ornamental shrubs and flowering bulbs, gorse, laburnum, lilacs, privet, trumpet trees, tulips, jonquils, hyacinths, daffodils, daisies and primroses as well as foxglove for medicinal purposes. These were packed in moss and despatched in boxes round Cape Horn.

Mary Ann James Shephard vividly remembered the trials of those pioneer days on Grand Mound prairie in the 1850s.[1] For instance, matches were almost unknown, and their first fires were produced with a flint and a box of tinder. As fire was precious, it was usual to light the domestic fire in the Fall in the main fireplace, and each night cover it carefully with ashes before going to bed. In the morning the ashes were raked out and dry tinder added until a strong blaze appeared. One cold morning no blaze appeared and the children had to remain in bed, no great hardship perhaps, until one of her brothers had run a mile or so to borrow fire from one of their Indian neighbours. Matches were a scarce and expensive commodity, 25 cents a dozen. At night firelight was supplemented by candles for general illumination. These were made in a double mould by Mary Ann herself. Her task was to thread the candle-wick through the mould, put a stick through the loops at the top, twist them, then tie them at the bottom, pour in the melted tallow and, when cold, cut the knots at the bottom, take hold of the stick and draw them out.

Restraining their livestock from wandering miles in all directions compelled the Jameses to fence their land with thousands of split wood rails. Unlike the stone hedgerows which framed the fields of his 500 acres at Trelan, Samuel had to depend on wedging into narrow rails the cedar trees which Indians helped him cut down. There were no great stones at hand for building walls and barbed wire fences were a device of the future. In a letter to Cornwall, Samuel said it required about five thousand split rails, 12 to 14 feet long, to make a mile of 'stake and rider' fencing. Woven in zig-zag fashion, these fences stood from eight to ten rails high, sufficient to confine horses and cattle and tight enough to keep sheep within.

> A man easily makes 100 rails in a day, some persons make from a 150 to 200, and it generally costs about as much time to handle them and put them up into a fence as it does to make them. To lay up 500 rails in a fence is reckoned a day's work. From 60 to 80 are generally handled on a wagon load and commonly from two to four loads are hauled in a day with an ox team.

It was slow and hard work but Samuel had four strong young sons who competed with each other to show who was best. And there were Indian men to help with felling trees and dragging rails to where needed.

In the summer of 1853, a large number of Indian families camped near the James house to gather wild berries and dig lacamas, an onion-like bulb which they dried as a wintertime food. One morning an Indian woman silently came to the James doorway and stood there until Samuel stepped out to ask what she wanted. Asking him to follow her, the Indian woman led Samuel to her hut in which her husband and three children lay with high fevers. He quickly recognized small pox, a dreaded disease which in past years had wiped out whole villages. 'We children were forbidden to go near their camp', Mary Ann remembered.

> One day Brother Richard and I had eaten a lot of elderberries and that evening Richard complained of being sick. Mother thought it was the berries but the next morning Richard was worse with bad head and back aches. Our nearest doctor was 100 miles away but Father knew the malady and we were forthwith dosed with 'James Pills' and given copious drinks of cream of tartar water and wild peppermint tea.
>
> Like a good captain preparing for a siege, Father prepared for every emergency. Three of my brothers were put in an out-building used as a workshop. A cowbell was hung near one of the beds to be rung if anything were needed. With the immunity gained through previously having had small pox, Father was our Doctor, Mother our trained nurse and Brother Thomas her assistant. We were all pretty sick children but in time we were up and well again, and not one of us pockmarked.

A night-time traveller who rode his horse up to the James house to ask for lodging wheeled away as if dodging lightning when Anna Maria explained her children had small pox. She stood in the doorway peering into the darkness as the clattering hoofbeats of the horse ridden by the apprehensive stranger dwindled away into the night.

Sick Indians too were being cared for at this time by Samuel. He managed to save most of them. One old chief who had two stricken sons begged Samuel to treat them as he had his own family, promising to give two horses if the boys lived unmarked. 'Father cured them both and the ponies were brought over,' wrote Mary Ann. 'Soon, however, one pony was missing and we found the chief had "borrowed" one back.'

According to her daughter, Anna Maria was a great favourite with the Indians and was successful in getting them to throw away an old custom. When a baby was born two small boards, padded with moss, were placed on its head, one at the front and the other at the back, and were held in position with thongs of deer sinew. Every few days these thongs were drawn a little tighter until the head was flattened, at which time the boards were removed. An Indian named Susunia asked Anna Maria to name his first child but she refused unless he promised not to flatten its head. It seems that he was pleased that his child would be the first of the tribe to have a natural head, and so Anna Maria obliged by naming him Adam.[2]

The Indians were so grateful for the medical attention Samuel gave them that a delegation came one day to tell him that he could have all the land on Grand Mound prairie, a gesture far more generous but less binding than the federal government's donation of 320 acres, signed by the President of the United States.

By the Fall of 1853 a large number of settlers had come north from lower Oregon to stake land claims on the prairies. Open land was appealing because it was free of the giant trees which the whites could remove only by burning. They had none of the long saws which loggers later brought in to fell the Douglas fir. The sight of smoke ribboning from the chimneys of new cabins 'only a few miles away' inspired Anna Maria to sing in her kitchen. A community was forming with a church and Sunday school for the children. Leonard Durgan brought several newcomers to consult with Samuel James about a name for the new settlement. Some had proposed 'Mt Vernon' in remembrance of the national hero, George Washington. Durgan, who now had a home on top of the Mound, asked Samuel if 'Grand Mound' would be an appropriate name. 'Of course,' said the first settler, 'of all the mounds in Oregon this is the grandest.' What had been called 'Big Mound' by some and merely 'The Mound' by others thus came to be known as Grand Mound. Within a year it boasted one of Washington Territory's first post offices.

Within a dozen miles of their home the Cornish could now count thirty new families who had come over the Oregon Trail from distant states. There were new names like Sarjent, Gangloff, Durgan, Baker, Tilley, Mills, Henness, Webster, Colvin, Sheal, Northcraft, Hogden, Crowder, Yantis, Brown and others of English, Scottish, Irish and German descent. Most of them were from families which had migrated into the United States anywhere from 50 to 100 years before. The Jameses at that time were the only local pioneers who had come directly from the 'old country'. Some of the new neighbours could read and write but many could not. Grown up without schooling, they signed documents with an 'X' mark, legally witnessed. The federal government required applicants to give written details about their backgrounds. Those who could not write came to Samuel James and he helped them prepare the written applications. Word soon got around that Samuel, who could also write in French, Greek and Latin, 'knew everything'. His counsel was sought for naming new communities. He made pills for the sick and pulled teeth when neighbours came to him with aching jaws, using the same nippers with which he removed harness rivets or yanked bent nails from boards. 'See the Englishman' was commonly advised when someone complained of feeling poorly or blinked unknowingly at words on paper or hungered for comforting quotations from the Bible. The yeoman farmer of Trelan in Cornwall had become a man of many trades and professions in his new world.

Things were gong well for Samuel as the wagons continued rolling into Washington in 1854. He now had a broad sweep of land as big as the farm he had left in Cornwall. His fields were fenced, the sheep and cattle were fattening and crop yields were better than he had ever known. 'Our sheep were doing well and we had soon increased our flocks to four or five hundred,' wrote John Rogers. 'When we wanted mutton, we killed a fat wether, shearing, washing and selling the wool at good prices. Often we would take a fat mutton to Olympia and the government officials would declare it was "the best mutton they had ever tasted". The prairie bunch grass was very nutritious. It produced good beef and mutton.'

Passers-by turned into the James place as if it were a way-station or a roadside inn, some of them important figures like Dr John McLoughlin, chief factor of the Hudson's Bay Company at Fort Vancouver and Dr William Fraser Tolmie, its surgeon. Samuel and Anna Maria welcomed travellers because they brought news from other settlements. One visitor was a little Frenchman named R. Brunn, who stopped over on his way to Grays Harbor. His packhorses were loaded with provisions and tools for farming. He had two little pigs lashed by their feet and balanced across a horse's back like saddlebags. Brunn said he was going to develop a townsite along the Chehalis River, which caused Samuel to smile and recall another town builder named Dudley back in Iowa where the Jameses had wintered in 1850–51. Brunn wanted to know the Greek words that meant 'City of the World'. Samuel told him 'Cosmo' meant the world and 'Polis' meant city. Brunn started Cosmopolis and at the turn of this century the town he founded boasted having the largest sawmill on the Pacific Coast.

Religious organisations flourished as the prairie population swelled. Prayer meetings were held in various homes and later came 'camp meetings' which attracted families to a wooded park-like place on Scatter Creek where they would remain a week or longer with preachers of various denominations voicing their tributes to the Creator mornings, afternoons and into the night. Women would work for days preparing food for the big outing. Anna Maria was noted for her good Cornish pies. The central theme of camp meetings was worship but the gatherings also had the effect of consolidating fellowhip among families which had shared in common the hardships of the Oregon Trail. This kindred feeling of community interest was to serve the pioneers well in the months ahead when tensions between the Indians and the new government of Washington Territory exploded into warfare which harassed the new settlements for nearly two years.

The federal act donating land to new settlers expired in 1854 and Washington's first territorial governor, Isaac Stevens, began parleys with the tribes to persuade them to give up claiming lands which the United States government had granted to whites. The Indians had none of the white man's notions about property titles. They insisted that all of the land was theirs now just as it had been before the first bewhiskered white poked his face into their presence. They were not troubled by the whites moving onto their lands. It was when they put up fences and told the natives to keep out that the Indians became resentful and restive. Governor Stevens sought to arrange treaties 'forever binding' which would assign the Indians to defined reservations in which they could govern themselves with help from the 'Great White Father'. He proposed payments for the land and offered hunting and fishing rights. Some tribes agreed to these treaties and some did not.

Not all opposition to the treaty provisions came from Indians. Some whites objected to what the government was offering. John Rogers said his father 'had very pronounced views regarding the treatment accorded by the white authorities to the native Indians. He considered it a great mistake to allot them reservations away from their fishing, hunting and grazing grounds and to send them to small uninhabitable places in the timber, totally changing their mode of living.'

In the midst of this treaty making, the Jameses learned that their own land claim was being considered by the Territory as a new reservation for the Chehalis Indians. Some of this was the same land which the Indians had 'given' to Samuel for doctoring them through the small pox epidemic in 1853.[3] One morning the Indian agent, Col. Michael T. Simmons, and several other territorial employees came riding in from Olympia to advise the Jameses to scoot out and locate elsewhere. Samuel was away at the time but tiny Anna Maria stiffened to her full height of five feet and, Cornish eyes flashing, told the Government official to find his reservation somewhere else. Fifteen-year-old John Rogers heard his Mother speak and he recalled 'The Colonel made the most sweeping bow we boys had ever seen from a man on horseback and as he turned in the saddle he said "Good day, Madam, I have advised you." When Father came home he hardly knew what to think of the bluff Mother had given the man who represented authority. Anyway, it passed off; the prairie continued to fill up rapidly. There was no more talk of a reservation at Grand Mound.'[4]

Indian problems were a dominant topic in the West in 1854 but to the eastward more ominous issues affecting the very life of the national union itself were festering among the States. The North and the South were approaching a blood-spilling rift over the issue of black slavery. The North opposed slavery on moral grounds; the South saw it as basic to its economy. Even at Grand Mound, thousands of miles west of the nearest slave plantations, the issue intensified as Southern pioneers argued with settlers from the North and a sprinkling of 'aliens' from other lands. Samuel James soon found himself surrounded by neighbours who totally disagreed with his views on the freedom of man—if that man were black.

The first political convention at Grand Mound was held in 1856 in Leonard Durgan's home atop the Mound.[5] Its objective was to determine the political affiliations of local property owners who were entitled to vote in Territorial elections. The 'Democrats' and the 'Whigs' were then the predominant political parties, but putting a halt to slavery was not one of their issues. When the meeting chairman asked those who were Whigs to stand on one side of the room and Democrats on the other, Samuel James stood alone as an Abolitionist, or 'Free Soiler', opposed to slavery. Finally a genial Scotsman named Andrew McCornack walked over and stood by the Cornishman. That demonstration of support, even though by only one man, influenced Samuel to work tirelessly against slavery in the years ahead. This steadfast tendency to stand up for his beliefs, even when greatly outnumbered, marked the life of Samuel James as a pioneer.

The first word of impending war with the Indians came in the Fall of 1854 from the east side of the Cascade Mountains. Some miners were reported to be surrounded by Indians who threatened to kill all of them. Alarmed at the quick spread of discontent among the eastern Washington natives, Governor Stevens sent a company of volunteers along with a company of regular troops to enforce his treaty demands. They got as far as the summit of the mountains when messengers overtook them with orders to return west at once. Indians organised into small bands had begun terrorising the settlers around Puget Sound. They killed one entire family and several other white individuals.[6] Word got around as fast as horsemen could ride. It soon reached the settlers at Grand Mound and on adjoining prairies. Quick to organise under the threat of being attacked, the settlers came to Grand Mound from miles around to discuss how to defend themselves. They quickly agreed on building a stockade into which they could flee if the new enemy broke through government troops who were sent to guard the mountain passes.

Military forts were hastily erected by the Territorial government near larger settlements. At Grand Mound the pioneers built their own haven. It was a stockade of logs 12 to 14 inches in diameter standing 12 feet high, with bastions or blockhouses mounted on two corners diagonally opposite so that riflemen could sweep all sides of the fort. The walls and inner buildings were completed within two weeks by volunteers with ox teams working from dawn to dark. Two wide gates for exit and entry were made from thick wood planks Samuel James had hauled from Armstrong's Mill at Cedar Creek to build his barn. Spaces were allotted along the inside walls for lean-to shacks in which the families could live. A well 15 feet deep for drinking and cooking water was dug and walled up with rock and a central guardhouse was built as a meeting place. A two-storey schoolhouse was added later.

Before the fort was occupied, a meeting of men and older boys who built the stockade was called to organise a military unit of volunteers who would serve with the regular army troops whenever called. Benjamin L. Henness was elected captain and the pioneers named their stockade 'Fort Henness'. John Rogers wrote: 'Brothers Samuel, 23, William, 21, and Thomas, 19, enlisted immediately. I was 15 and wanted to enlist, too, but Father held me back, saying he wanted to keep one son at home. I was enrolled with the "home guard" as we had to leave someone to protect the women and children when the volunteers were out scouting.' The government at Olympia supplied muskets, ammunition and blankets for the militia. Samuel James drew five muskets for himself and four older sons. 'I was very proud of my musket with its long bayonet,' said John Rogers. 'I would often leave the fort after standing my four hours night guard duty and walk across the prairie three miles to get the sheep out of the pasture early in the morning. We had to keep them corralled from the coyotes at night.'

In 1855–56 Fort Henness was to be a refuge for 227 men, women and children for sixteen months. They came and went as word of critical hostilities reached them. When the pressure was off, the families returned to their homes. Messengers raced from farm to farm spreading the alarm when Indian threats were renewed. A sign of danger was the ringing of a bell hung upon a high post.

For some time Indian families that had always lived near Grand Mound were allowed to remain. They were friendly to the whites because the Cornish and other settlers had treated them fairly and won their trust. 'Hostile Indians from other areas would come onto the prairie after dark,' recalled John Rogers. 'They would shout and holler "Who ho, who ho," trying to entice local Indians out to trouble us. Boys and older men not in the volunteer service became the home guards. We would go and come from our home places, looking after the stock and getting produce from the fields and gardens. We took some chances of being waylaid by the "salix tillicum," the fighting Indians, who frequented the countryside.'

As fighting increased, the settlers and government thought it best to assemble the Chehalis tribe at the home of Judge Sidney Ford six miles north of Grand Mound. The Chehalis gave up their muskets and the firing locks were removed. To protect these friendly natives from warring Indians a small guard of volunteers remained at Ford's place. The government supplied beef and other provisions for the Indians in this camp. The Chehalis were given permits to go see their friends down the river but were required to carry a white flag of truce while on the trail. John Rogers saw many of them riding on the run across the prairie, waving their truce flag on a stick. 'It was amusing to hear some of the fort guards shout out threats when a red handkerchief was tied to the end of a stick. I knew these Indians well and excused their ignorance in flaunting a red flag instead of white in these warlike times.'

One night after his usual four-hour guard duty, John Rogers walked from the fort to his home aware of hearing more than the usual number of Indian night calls.

> I began to think it might not be safe to sleep in our house while guarding the sheep and reasoned, boy-like, that a bunch of hogs that were sleeping in the open shed of the barn would scent the Indians if any came near . . . Pigs would usually rush and snort when Indians came near them. I wrapped my overcoat around me and clasped my faithful old army musket in my arms. I remained near the pigs but did not need a stampede to keep me awake. The groans and grunts and squeals, together with the despicable smell, was enough.

Samuel, William and Thomas James served out their enlisted term with the volunteers but when it came for them to re-enlist the elder Samuel James objected to his boys serving any longer. He reasoned that the regular army troops were sufficient to quell any further disturbances in Western Washington and that Fort Henness volunteers should not have to fight Indians on the east side of the Cascade mountains where no white settlements except a couple of army posts existed. This position by Samuel won him no popularity among the families that wanted to chase Indians to the end of the earth and punish them without mercy. The Jameses moved out of the fort in 1856 and remained on their farm except when hostilities renewed. On these occasions they would move into the Durgan house on top of the Mound, where they felt as safe as in the nearby stockade.

Some Indian-haters tried to pin a murder charge on Samuel James to discredit him with his native friends. Some referred to him as 'the hated Englishman' because he was outspoken for human freedom, defended his black friend, George Bush, and campaigned against political parties which advocated retaining slavery in America. John Rogers described the incident:[7]

> Our people were Abolitionists and Independent Methodists without racial prejudice, leaning to free trade principles and opposed to secret organisation. Now maybe you don't think we had some unpleasant times with people who thought otherwise. We young people were returning from the fort to the home place one Sunday when we saw two men of the baser sort running away from our place.
>
> When we came to our gate we found a bottle with some Whisky in it and an Indian's riding whip. We took them into the house to show Father and Brother Samuel who were reading. That evening we learned an Indian had been killed near our place. Neighbouring Indians identified the whip as belonging to the dead man. Father investigated and immediately surmised what had happened. The white men we had seen leaving our place were seen at times with a camp of Indians that came to pick berries. The young Indian victim had come from another camp to find his wife, who had been enticed away from him. The plotters, pretending to be friends, got him drunk, persuaded him to walk out on a log extending over the river bank, then pushed him off. The fall broke his neck. The plot to get our family into trouble with the natives backfired. Investigators absolved us of any blame and the local Indians came to assure us they knew who had done the evil deed.

Thieving was common on the prairies and whites were just as guilty as Indians. Sheep were frequently stolen from the Jameses, who had hundreds in their flocks. Some who disliked the abolitionist Samuel thought it clever to pilfer his wagons going to market at Olympia. John Rogers described one occasion when a group of rowdies overtook a wagon loaded with what one said was butter owned by 'Old Man James'. Butter from one churn looks like butter from any other. The thief learned later that the butter he took from the wagon belonged to his own mother.

Fort Henness was not called upon to repulse any attacks in the 1855–56 Indian War. No red-skinned battalions stormed its sharp-pointed palisades. Yet one native died when shot by a guard. The victim was a young Chehalis Indian who had ridden from Judge Ford's home on a Sunday to visit people he knew in the fort. Friendly Indians had been provided with a white flag to display when approaching Fort Henness. The guard who saw this youth coming swore he displayed no flag so he shot him. When whites rushed out to examine the Indian they found a small white flag clutched in his hand. A general uprising of the Chehalis Indians who were outraged by the shooting was avoided only when territorial authorities jailed the guard who did the shooting and confined him until after the war. In contrast with the over-reaction by the whites was an incident when four white boys, eight to ten years old, were permitted out of the fort one afternoon to pick wild strawberries. They wandered into a wooded area and heard horsemen approaching. The boys hid under bushes and when the riders went by threw some wild cucumbers at them. The riders were hostile Indians who, wheeling around, found the 'enemy' to be little boys. Giving 'war whoops', they grinned at the boys and rode away into the forest.

During the months of 'siege' parents within the fort organised Grand Mound's first school. Samuel provided inspiration for this with the hundreds of books he had brought from Cornwall. A two-storey building set up for the school inspired Masonic Lodge members to use the upper room as a 'temple'. This touched off a hot debate between the lodge members and Samuel, who did not want the school and a secret order so closely associated. He argued that the Masons should put up their own hall. As a compromise, the Masons agreed to insulate the space between their lodge room and the schoolroom below with tan bark from a newly-started prairie tannery. John Rogers, one of the older pupils, recalled that the insulation worked perfectly, 'because even when the children pressed their ears to the walls they couldn't hear anything the lodgemen said or did'.

Today's only witness to those trying times in Fort Henness in 1855–56 is a fenced acre belonging to the Washington State Historical Society, which has erected a granite marker on the site. This stands on the other side of a country road only a few paces from the pioneer cemetery in which Samuel and Anna Maria James and some sixty of their descendants are buried.

NOTES

1. Journal of Mary Ann James Shephard (1911), quoted in David James, *Grand Mound to Scatter Creek*, pp. 29–30.

2. David James, p. 30.
3. Ibid., p. 41.
4. Autobiography of John Rogers James (1916).
5. David James, p. 31.
6. Journal of Mary Ann James Shephard (1911), quoted in David James, pp. 32–5.
7. Autobiography of John Rogers James (1916).

CHAPTER 12

Downstream to Lone Rock

Treaties prepared and imposed upon the Indians by the federal government's superior fire power served to lessen the worries of white settlers in Washington Territory after 1866. The unhappy natives retreated into reservations poorly suited to their migratory life styles. 'Rights' assigned to them for hunting and fishing were not to be realised until more than a century later when the Supreme Court of the United States upheld the validity of treaties long ignored by white people.

In the months of hostilities which had kept pioneer families cowering behind the log palisades of Fort Henness on Grand Mound prairie, Samuel James had ample time to look back upon his experiences and evaluate them. He had now lived 14 years in America. He was 52 years old. He had moved three times over incredible distances, crossing an ocean and an untamed continent to settle his wife and eight children 'in a land where there is the least possibility of future wars'. In the years since arriving at Grand Mound in 1852, he and his family had acquired enough land to provide good support. He had built a large home and farm site. He and his sons had fenced in their sheep flocks and cattle herds. Beyond their zig-zag split cedar rail fences they could see the chimney smoke of other pioneer settlers who had come to the treeless prairies. Samuel had welcomed these newcomers as helpful co-builders of the community. Yet Samuel also saw future limitations on opportunities for his growing sons and daughters. Free government land was less available. He took notice of other regions opening to settlers.

New land was not Samuel's only concern. Also on his mind were the grinding forces of political differences over state's rights and the inhuman practice of black slavery. These were the issues that were to simmer, seethe and finally flame into the fury of a civil war which blood-drained the nation between 1861 and 1865. The land of peace to which Samuel aspired when he left Cornwall was souring into a cauldron of hatred and reprisal. Samuel kept up with national events through subscriptions to New York periodicals. He read the Portland, Oregon, and Olympia, Washington Territory, newspapers and frequently expressed his views in letters to the editors. One letter he wrote to the *Pioneer and Democrat* of Olympia was concerned with his position on the slavery issue. It was published on 2 September 1854 and is interesting for the boldness of his arguments and the clarity with which he expressed them. He began by enunciating 'the great principle of natural law applicable to man in a state of society', that no man should injure another and that every man should 'to the utmost of his power' do everything to prevent one man being injured by another. It thus followed, he argued, that every man who is deprived of his personal liberty and made the slave of another suffers 'one of the greatest, most complicated and entire wrongs that it is possible for a human being to endure'. He has nothing left to him of all the 'inalienable rights' with which his Creator endowed him.

This led Samuel to tackle the question that was uppermost in people's minds: 'If slavery becomes eventually annihilated, what is to be done with the black coloured and degraded African race?' His critics had challenged him whether he would want to let them loose and so 'finally bring about the destruction of the superior qualities and endowments of the Anglo-Saxon race'. Not at all, he wrote emphatically. There were two possibilities. One was to allocate to the blacks certain areas of the American continent, so that they could form new states for their own exclusive use. The other was the one Samuel preferred, that of absorption into the European communities, even though this was the more difficult and the consequences unpredictable. But he was positive that the evils 'likely to arise from hurtful amalgamation among the two races (white and black) if living in one community' were exaggerated.

As slavery issues grew more controversial, it did not take long for the Jameses to learn that as dissenters they were a minority among their neighbours who had come from slave-holding states. These settlers upheld the right of whites to own black people as property. Influenced by a desire to remove himself from these controversies, Samuel began thinking of a new migration. Westward down the Chehalis River from Grand Mound lay new lands. Land meant the Jameses could expand their beef cattle herds and sheep flocks which were prospering at Grand Mound. Samuel saw possibilities of new homes for his older sons. The oldest, Samuel, was satisfied with his situation at the Mound but William, Thomas and John Rogers urged their Father to 'take a look downstream'.

In September 1857 Samuel and Anna Maria joined several other Mound couples in planning an exploration of Grays Harbor. At the last moment three wives backed out, leaving Anna Maria as the only woman to go boating down the river with her husband and sons, William, 21, and John Rogers, 17. With them were two Methodist preachers named Byles and Goodell; Michael Luark, an independent-minded pioneer; and a Byles son named David. Led by an Indian guide, Susunia, and his wife, the party paddled canoes nearly 70 miles in two days, arriving on a Saturday in the harbour where the Chehalis River spills into the Pacific Ocean. Next day, the two Methodists preached the first Sunday sermons ever heard on the harbor which Yankee navigator Capt. Robert Gray had discovered in 1792.[1]

Anna Maria became aware of a new Indian superstition when the party decided to cross the nine-mile-wide harbor in a large Indian canoe. Midway to their destination Susunia's wife discovered Anna Maria was holding some round clam shells she had picked up on the beach as pretty souvenirs. Horrified, because they believed clam shells in a canoe meant bad luck, the Indians insisted they would turn back unless the shells were dumped overboard. So Anna Maria tossed away her shells and ruefully watched them sink, thus avoiding what might have been the first labour strike in Washington Territory.

The Grand Mound expedition spent two weeks on Grays Harbor, sizing up desirable land locations. Samuel and his son, William, each filed applications for 160 acres adjoining on the north shore. Offshore, fronting their property, stood a kettle-shaped redstone pillar which they dubbed 'Lone Rock'. This isolated pillar, rising 75 feet, could be seen from all parts of the inner harbor. It has since become known as James Rock in memory of the first white family to establish a home in that part of Grays Harbor. Samuel was pleased with this new site. It gave him a view of the surging waves of the Pacific Ocean remindful of the Atlantic pounding the fringes of the Lizard peninsula within sound of Trelan farm. He had not given up Grand Mound. He was now in a position to have two homes and more grass-rich acreage for the livestock he and his sons were building into sizeable herds.

The Chehalis River linked Grand Mound and Grays Harbor in this early time before roads could be cut through the massive Douglas fir forests which cloaked the entire Chehalis Valley. Mary Ann James, then 10 years old, went down the river with her parents on a trip to Lone Rock in the Spring of 1858. She recalled:[2]

> Soon after we had reached Lone Rock, William also came down to help Father build a log cabin as our first shelter. Not a nail was used. The logs were mortised together; rafters were fastened by means of wooden pegs and the clapboards for the roof were tied on with withes from hazelnut bushes. I carried the clapboards up a ladder to cover the house while Father and William were cutting wild hay for the cattle they intended to drive over trails through the woods from Grand Mound in the Fall.

The brothers William and John stayed in the new Lone Rock cabin through a wet and lonesome 1858–9 winter. But they were young and the duck-hunting was so fabulous that they were content. The year 1859 also brought new

---

Opposite: *Gray's Harbor at the mouth of the Chehalis River, with the site of Samuel James's homestead on the shore of the bay and, offshore, the James Rock, a Columbian redstone pillar 75 feet high, accessible at low tide. All that remains of the settlement are apple trees, still bearing fruit.* Photograph Jones Photo Co., Aberdeen, Washington

experiences to Ann Eliza James, now an eligible 16 and so pretty that young men—and older ones, too—swirled for a second look when she passed by. 'Girls were very scarce and bachelors were a surplus commodity', wrote Mary Ann, aptly observing the attentions received by her older sister. 'I am sure you will scarcely believe me when I tell you Eliza had 50 bonafide offers of marriage.'

> She was only 13 when a six-foot Polander, who knew if he had a wife he could file for 320 acres instead of 160, approached Father with his plans. Father stiffened, glowered and showed him the door. Another suitor wrote that he had enough lumber on the ground for a house, one horse, a barrel of meat and other groceries, a pair of willing hands, a good heart, etc. But that didn't impress Eliza. One poor fellow was so broken-hearted over her refusing him that he went to California and wrote his own obituary, sending it to the Olympia newspaper. In time his heart mended and he found another girl who took him. Men were desperate for marriage. I knew one man who asked three different girls the same day. With many men it was a case of 'Anybody, Lord'.

Mary Ann recalled the time a hopeful Scotsman, aged 49, came to the family home to propose to Eliza:

> They were in the parlor. Our walls were not plastered so I could hear pretty well from the kitchen where Mother was stirring up a pudding. She asked me to hold the bag while she poured the batter in. This happened just as I overheard the man in the parlor say to Eliza 'Will ye ha me?' I snickered loudly and dropped the pudding bag. Mother boxed my ears good for that but I noticed her eyes twinkled as she slapped at me. And Eliza didn't 'ha him'.

The family's travels up and down the river were delightful camping trips to the smaller children. The parents knew the danger of submerged logs and swift riffles where the water swirled and boiled around sunken snags. Low-hanging tree branches hovering over bends in the river often swept unwary people out of their shallow dugout canoes. One party of federal soldiers and their families had upset in a dangerous rapid and only the swimming skill of Indian guides saved the mothers and children from drowning. Canoe paddlers could easily go from Grand Mound to the harbour in a single day if the tide was ebbing at the lower end; otherwise, the journey took two days. It was a three-day pull upstream in summer months when the river levels dropped, forcing men to pole their canoes through shallow waters. When the craft rubbed the gravel bottom, everybody climbed out and waded, pulling the canoe to deeper water. Mary Ann remembers the beauty of the boating scene:

> As night came, a suitable landing was found, the canoe pulled up high and dry on a sand bar and camp was made. We never had a tent. A big tree was chosen as a shelter under which we slept. After the camp fire was made, the men fried bacon and cooked pancakes which they expertly flipped by giving the pan a toss up high so the 'flapjack' could be caught as it turned coming down.

She also recalled a favourite camping place at the mouth of the Satsop river, one of several tributaries flowing into the Chehalis, where one could always find a number of Indians and the finest salmon and trout fishing anywhere on the journey.

> After a salmon was caught it would be cleaned and split down the back. The bones were removed. A sharpened stick was thrust in the length of the fish and stuck in the ground upright in front of hot coals. The sticks were turned until the salmon was a delicate brown. We baked potatoes in the hot ashes at the same time. It was more like a feast than a meal. Our blankets were laid on a soft spot in the sand and we were soon asleep, being awakened early in the morning by the gently rippling of the water over the stones and the twittering and singing of many birds.

A memorable river meeting took place between Anna Maria James and a nephew, Harry Gartrell, who, unbeknownst to her, had come to America from the Lizard in Cornwall. Mary Ann described the scene:

> Harry had arrived at Grand Mound just as we were leaving for Grays Harbor. So we invited him to come along. Mother was then at the Harbor and we assumed she would be there when we arrived. We had no idea she was at the very time coming back to Grand Mound. We were lazily drifting down the river, heading toward a long riffle which the men were preparing to wade and pull the boat over. Harry had one shoe and sock off when I looked downstream and saw Mother wading up the riffle ahead of two Indians who were pulling her canoe. I shouted 'Mother!' and Harry jumped out of our canoe, one shoe on and one shoe off, to wade splashingly right into Mother's amazed embrace.

It was the first time they had seen each other since the Jameses' departure from Cornwall 15 years earlier.

Later in 1859, Samuel and his sons built a freight raft of large fir timbers on the river bank at Grand Mound and launched it loaded with lumber, nails, shingles, tools and other essentials for building a new home at Lone Rock. They floated and poled their way down the Chehalis, beached at the Rock place and built a comfortable two-storey dwelling which Samuel and Anna Maria occupied for the next five years. The raft was taken apart and its huge timbers became foundations for the house.

Among the many young men who came to Chehalis Point on the harbour mouth opposite Lone Rock was a slender fellow named Frank McKee Stocking. He was sailing a small sloop one day when a hard storm came up suddenly, capsizing the boat and forcing Stocking and two companions to hang on for their lives. They clung to the boat bottom throughout one night and at dawn, nearly dead from exposure, were rescued by Indians. Brought to the James home to get dry clothing and recover from his chills, Frank Stocking met Eliza James for the first time. He liked what he saw and she liked what she saw. On 19 February 1861 they were united in the James house, the first wedding on Grays Harbor. Ever the observer, Mary Ann described her sister's wedding:

> The bride wore a white tarleton dress. The wedding presents were not very numerous but quite acceptable: a cow, a calf, a little dog, some household linen and bedding and a deed to 60 acres of land at the mouth of the Satsop River. As we were all seated and the bridal couple entered the room the dog began barking

> furiously at something outside the front door. We heard a piteous little cry. Father, who was seated near the door, hastily opened it and in jumped a little five-year-old Indian boy dressed in nothing but a little shirt, which we quickly noticed was too short. Before Father could stop him, the boy was standing in the middle of the room and there he stood until the preacher concluded the ceremony. It was different and it kept us from crying. Mother asked the boy who had sent him and he said his uncle, an Indian named Oqully, had told him to come. Oqully came to our place later in the day. When Mother learned the boy's parents were dead she asked Oqully to give her the little tot. He agreed. Mother got ready a hot bath, gave the boy a good scrubbing, cut down a shirt and pants belonging to Brother Richard and dressed him as her newest son. Father immediately named him Sampson because he was so muscular. Sampson lived with us until he was 14, a bright and happy boy. Consumption was then a common illness among Indians. Sampson died of consumption in 1870 and we mourned him as much as if he had been born into our family.

As the years of civil war spread violence and suffering across America, life for the Jameses had periods of suspense from events far removed from battlefields east of the Rocky Mountains. Squalls racing suddenly across Grays Harbor frequently proved disastrous to home-built craft attempting to sail its waters. The Jameses managed safe voyages in an eight-ton sloop they had built at Grand Mound for journeys on the river and even out to sea. Their sloop was named 'Olive Branch' after his sons persuaded Samuel it was less flamboyant than the title 'Anti-War' he had scrawled across its bow with a grease swab. It was his manner of expressing disapproval of the civil war.[3] It was when they set forth in rowboats or flat-bottomed scows that storms threatened them. John Rogers recalled two harrowing sea experiences. One was when he and his father were rowing from Chehalis Point homeward with a new iron kitchen stove as cargo. The stove had been ordered from San Francisco, California, as a special present for Anna Maria. 'Halfway home, the winds turned, heavy seas came up and to save ourselves from swamping we had no choice but to dump the stove overboard', John Rogers wrote, adding that his Mother concealed her regrets with exclamations over how happy she was to get them home alive.

Another time, John Rogers, Harry Gartrell, and the newlyweds, Francis and Eliza James Stocking, were sailing a scow, a flat-bottomed boat with square ends, toward Chehalis Point with a heifer calf as cargo. Eliza's little dog also was aboard. Tides turned and the anchor dropped to hold the scow broke loose. Helpless against tidal powers, the party was swept over the breakers of Grays Harbor bar. Smashing waves broke the scow's railing. The calf fell overboard and drowned and the crew, bailing to save themselves from sinking, survived only because ocean currents turned them back toward the shore. Michael Luark, who had been a member of the Grand Mound expedition to the harbour in 1857, chanced to be riding horseback along the shore. He sighted the swamped scow, bravely rode his horse into the surf to get a line attached and pulled the craft to safety. Eliza's dog had not waited to be rescued. It leaped overboard and swam ashore to shake itself dry on the beach.

Pleasant relationships between the family and Indians on Grays Harbor led to the tribal people naming Anna Maria 'Tenas La-me-ah', meaning 'Little Mother'. Samuel's rugged Cornish features and prominent Roman nose won him the name 'Colowax', meaning 'Big Nose'. Anna Maria won the confidence of the Indians through many instances of sympathy and understanding.[4] Typical was an event occurring at the outbreak of the civil war. A white man was murdered at Chehalis Point and Indians were blamed by white authorities. The accused Indians protested their innocence. Finally, because of the still sensitive feelings between the races, Governor Isaac Stevens came from Olympia to make his own study of the murder. Lacking an understanding of English, the native chief asked Anna Maria to go with his people to put their case before the Big White Chief. Daughter Mary Ann accompanied her mother when two big canoes filled with solemn Indians beached at Lone Rock to pick them up for the journey.

> Imagine if you can, a small woman wearing a plum colored bonnet and a gray shawl, the points just touching the ground, walking over the sand at Chehalis Point, followed by a large number of Indian men into the hotel where Governor Stevens was to see them. Mother explained to the Governor her reason for being there; the Indians made good their case and were dismissed. Governor Stevens then told Mother if she were a man he would appoint her the General Indian Agent.

The murderer never was apprehended but it was commonly believed that another white, not Indians, had committed the crime.

Mary Ann's journals included two other unusual experiences. One involved a day when Samuel had sailed to nearby Hoquiam community with his sons to work on land which John Rogers had acquired, leaving Mary Ann and her mother alone at the Rock place. Sensing visitors nearby, Mary Ann looked out of a window and saw several large canoes landing.

> I do not know how many Indians there were but they were all men, most of them wearing blankets, and all had guns and knives. I was frightened and Mother, who was afraid of nothing, looked a little pale, for we quickly saw they were not local Indians. Mother stood by the kitchen table and I behind her as the strangers came in, filling the room. Speaking Chinook jargon, Mother asked who they were. They said they were Makah Indians from the northern part of the Olympic Peninsula. Local Indians feared the Makahs, who sometimes staged raids and stole their women as slaves. They told Mother they had brought their canoes down the Ocean coast and they had sea otter skins for sale. They asked where our men were. Mother said they were nearby. The fierce-looking leader asked if we were afraid. Mother, brave little mother, replied 'No, we are not afraid. We trust in the Lord Jesus and he protects us.' Then she mentioned to me to play our melodion. I sat down and played a famous tune, 'John Brown's Body', with all my might.
>
> You should have seen the Makahs. Some got down on their hands and knees, looking to see where the music came from. They were both mystified and pleased. Before leaving, they offered me three otter skins (worth $500 to $800 in the market). Some took off rings and bracelets and gave them to me. They went away praising my music and for once I felt like a 'star'. I remember Mother standing in

> the doorway, watching the grim Makahs paddle away with their swaying rhythmic strokes. All she said was 'mercy me'.

Samuel James treated Indians as the true owners of the land to which white pioneers were given title through the federal government's laws. At Grand Mound and again at Grays Harbor he made agreements with local chiefs before considering he had full title both within the law and within his conscience. Before building his home at Lone Rock, Samuel took Anna Maria, William, and Mary Ann with him to meet Mr Mootles, the aged chief of Indians living on nearby Chanouse Creek. Mr Mootles had acquired his name from Hudson's Bay Company trappers and he was proud of it, especially of being called 'Mister'. Samuel took along flour, sugar, calicos and lots of trade beads as a present to Mr Mootles. Mary Ann described the meeting:

> Mr Mootles ruled over a large Indian village. We walked in to find men lying and sitting around in the sunshine. Some were playing 'chill-chill', a gambling game. Some of their women were weaving mats and baskets. Others were spinning wool gathered from mountain thickets, torn from the sheep as they browsed for grass. We were watching them spin and weave when Chanouse, the chief's fine looking son, came to take us to his father. The chief's house was 40 or 50 feet long and 20 feet wide. It was made of split cedar boards and bark. An opening along the ridge pole let out smoke from the open fires.
>
> An oval door hung from the top by buckskin thongs. We pushed the door to one side and stepped over the threshold. Inside, all around the walls, was a raised platform about five feet wide, covered with bark mats. Family belongings such as blankets, chests and baskets of all shapes and sizes were stowed along the walls. The baskets were so tightly woven they held water without leaking. To heat water, the women dropped hot stones into the filled baskets. The nicely made wood chests were filled with dishes, calico cloths and beads that had come from Hudson's Bay Company traders.
>
> A fire in the middle of the room was tended by an old woman who cooked fish or whatever they were eating that day. In other houses occupied by two or more families, each family would have its own fire going. On this warm day the fire in the chief's house was only smouldering, banked to keep it going because the Indians rarely let their house fires die out. Mr Mootles, who was very old, sat at the far end of the house. A number of young women and men sat near him. We all shook hands with the chief. Father and William placed their presents at his feet. 'Marsy' [Thank You] said Mr Mootles as he mentioned to us to be seated upon mats facing him. Father made a little speech which Chanouse translated for his father, who did not understand either Chinook or English. Mr Mootles replied through his son that the land we had settled upon was ours forever and that he was our friend.
>
> Then he spoke to the young Indian women, who went to one of the trunks and took out some very pretty blue plates and wooden spoons, giving each of us a plate and a spoon. One of the girls brought a small basket and poured onto our plates a fine lot of salmon berries and then—oh dear!—she brought a blue and white jug and poured whale oil over the berries. We discreetly ate the oily berries, picking and nibbling and smacking our lips. Mr Mootles seemed very pleased that we so enjoyed this delicacy. He told us how much he liked our presents and invited us to come to see him again.

As he sat on his porch facing Lone Rock and listening to the distant pounding of the ocean waves, Samuel James will often have thought of the struggles he and Anna Maria had made in their new homeland. He will not have been disappointed. His sons were young men, well prepared for careers they would follow in farming, business and government service. Daughter Eliza had married a young Easterner who adapted quickly to Western ways. Mary Ann, the only child to receive a formal education, was ready to enter a private school in Victoria, B.C., then the cultural centre of the burgeoning Northwest. In January 1863 President Abraham Lincoln had issued his Emancipation Proclamation, freeing all black slaves. This accomplished a purpose Samuel had supported in his years as an Abolitionist when the threat of slavery loomed in the new Oregon country.

At Lone Rock, as he had at Grand Mound and at Milwaukie, Oregon, and earlier in Caledonia, Wisconsin, Samuel planted acres of fruit orchards. Survivors among his apple trees at Lone Rock bear fruit to this day, 125 years after the original seedlings were put into the ground. He fenced in the tidal prairies to contain the beef cattle he, William and John Rogers were raising in combination with son Samuel's thriving herds at Grand Mound. The Jameses were supplying beef and mutton to Victoria markets by boat shipments through Olympia.

Samuel's sight and hearing remained good as he neared his 60th birthday. One summer day in 1864 the greying Cornish pioneer became ill from a stroke while working in his fields. Anna Maria described the incident in a letter to her brother, John Foxwell, in Wisconsin:[5]

> It was while finishing a hedge or ditch fence on the tidal prairie to rescue grass lands from the tidal overflows that Samuel suddenly felt as if he had been struck a heavy blow on the head. From that time on he was never again well. I had often remarked to Father that in that hedge he had built a monument to himself. Alas, I little thought then of how close I was to the truth.
>
> The place never looked so beautiful as it looked that Spring of 1864. A pang goes through my heart when I think of our much-loved spot. I visited it last summer and wept aloud as I wandered through the weed-grown garden and looked at the trees laden with fruit, the ground strewed thick with apples and the currants black and red on the bushes. I visited the haunts and places I had often enjoyed with him who was to visit them no more. One was a spot which resembled our place in Cornwall and which Father called 'Kabbua'.[6]

Too ill to remain in the isolation of Lone Rock, Samuel James was brought back up the Chehalis River to his Grand Mound farm. He died on 28 January 1866 in his 61st year and was buried in Grand Mound's resting place for pioneers, only a stone's toss from the decaying walls of the Fort Henness he had helped to build a decade earlier. The horse-drawn farm wagon which carried his cedar coffin from the farm across the prairie to the burial was followed on foot by a procession of the pioneer neighbours who also had known the hardships and triumphs of the Oregon Trail. Behind them came another group, the Indian neighbours whose friendship and trust he had won through respect and kindness. It was a sunny day and the prairie grass rippled in westerly breezes. The long journey of Samuel James from Trelan on the Lizard Peninsula to the prairies of Western Territory had ended.

NOTES

1. Edwin Van Syckle, *The River Pioneers*, p. 30.
2. Journal of Mary Ann James Shephard (1911).
3. David James, *Grand Mound to Scatter Creek*, pp. 41–4.
4. Ibid., p. 41.
5. This letter of Anna Maria is dated 23 March 1866 and addressed from Grand Mound, Thurston County, Washington. It is the last one of hers to survive.
6. It is not clear what Samuel James meant by 'Kabbua'. Perhaps he had said at some time 'Kabbalah', the Hebrew word which signifies hidden wisdom or grace in the sense that God is boundless. It would be within Samuel's experience to choose a word which indicated that God lived in such a place. On the other hand he may have meant 'Kaaba', the sacred Moslem Shrine at Mecca which contained a black stone supposed to have been given to Abraham by the archangel Gabriel.

CHAPTER 13

The Cornish-American Legacy

Anna Maria James spent her remaining 13 years at Grand Mound in the home of her eldest son Samuel, died in 1879 aged 73 and was buried at the side of her husband in the pioneer cemetery. With their deaths there came to an end an episode of pioneering which has no parallel in the history of Cornish emigration. It marked the completion of the transition from being born Cornish to dying American. Only once did Samuel ever return to Cornwall, and Anna Maria and their children never. The family became totally American, tied to the land and the gospel of labour which tamed a wilderness. In the Pacific North-West Samuel acquired in 1852 a single 320-acre land grant which, enlarged through purchases, he shared with each of his sons and daughters. They in turn shared their lands with their children. Thus by 1900 the original holder had grown into a community of 16 adjoining holdings, all owned by members of the same family and known as Jamestown.[1]

Land and family were at the heart of Samuel's quest, not land that might form the nucleus of an agricultural empire nor land in any part of the United States so long as it was productive, but land that was always in the West. Four times in twenty years he pulled up his stakes until he came to rest on the shores of the Pacific, as if he were mystically and symbolically forever walking into a sunset. Nor were these moves hastily conceived. They were deliberately and carefully planned, almost as if he were drawn onwards by some spiritual magnet.

The United States fascinated, beckoned and attracted him as it had done many a Cornishman before. One has only to think of Charles Morton, the son of the vicar of St Ives, who in 1685 became the Vice-President of Harvard, or Jonathan Hornblower who built the first steam-engine in the United States in 1753 in New Jersey and represented that state in the Congress of the Confederation in 1785. On the other hand, Samuel invites comparison with other men from the extreme west of Cornwall who, a generation earlier, had made their mark on national life in their own individual ways: Davies Gilbert and Humphry Davy, both

Presidents of the Royal Society; Richard Trevithick, whose attempt to save the silver mines of South America is an epic in itself; and all those miners and engineers who left Cornwall in 1824 in the employ of the entrepreneur John Taylor to dry out the flooded mines of Mexico after winning its independence from Spain. Samuel carried within himself something of the cosmopolitanism of all Cornishmen.

National fame Samuel did not pursue, though one perhaps should not forget George Eliot's observation at the end of her novel *Middlemarch*: 'the growing good of the world is partly dependent on historic acts; and that things are not so ill with me as they might have been is half owing to the numbers who lived faithfully in hidden life and rest in unvisited tombs.' To live faithfully to his principles was certainly one of Samuel's qualities and he rarely sought publicity. Those principles were derived from a belief in a personal God and in a Christianity independent of religion, which Samuel had found lacking in Cornwall. In building a dissenting church which retained the episcopate of the Church of England, he felt that Methodists were departing from the original spirit of Christianity. What he advocated was an arrangement of independent local organisations such as obtained in apostolic times, like the churches at Antioch and Ephesus. Thus in Washington Territory, where all was virgin soil, he believed he had found the spiritual soil in which to seed these notions. The missionaries who were soon on the scene in the wake of Samuel's wagons he urged to get together in some kind of fellowship to conduct services in non-sectarian form. Among them was the Revd George Whitworth who later was to found in Spokane the college that bears his name, where to this day the kind of Christianity practised is that which Samuel once advanced.[2]

Furthermore, Samuel was opposed to fraternal organisations like the Free Masons and the Oddfellows on the grounds that they were opposed to the very spirit of Christianity in a free society. Again he did not believe in infant baptism, maintaining that this was purely a matter of individual choice, to be decided in adult life and by no means a condition of entry for church membership. He claimed that his Christian ethics were supported by the two great principles of natural law: no man should do an injury to another; and every man should be required to the utmost of his powers to prevent one man injuring another and to render him every assistance in his distress. It is not surprising therefore to find Samuel an early critic of slavery and of federal governments that dumped Indians on reservations away from their fishing, hunting, and grazing grounds. In his dealings with both Indians and Africans, he always treated them as equals, to the annoyance of new settlers from the East, and especially when he

---

Opposite: *The James family at Grand Mound in the early 1870s. Standing, from the left, Mary Ann Frances, John Rogers, Richard Oregon, Samuel II, Eliza and William. Seated, from the left, Mrs John Rogers, Anna Maria and Mrs Samuel II.* Photograph by courtesy of David James

shook them by the hand or visited local chiefs for permission to settle on land which was traditionally theirs but had been appropriated by the federal government.

To discover some Eldorado of precious metals was never a factor in Samuel's thinking. He seems to have had no interest at all in Cornwall's own extractive industries, nor in the lead mines of Wisconsin, nor in the miners he met on the trail to Oregon who were heading for California, even going so far as to argue with one of his sons against joining them. Thus the emigration of those farming families from the Lizard, the Moyles, the Foxwells and the Jameses, all connected by marriage, was completely untypical of the general exodus of the Cornish to the United States in the nineteenth century, and the experience of the Jameses was even more exceptional for they were the only ones to move west along the Oregon Trail. The tin and copper miners of Cornwall were pushed out to seek a better life in the United States because of the closing of the mines through periodic falls in metal prices. The general pattern was for the young men to go off hopefully to seek a fortune and then to return home to invest in Cornish mines. But the Jameses never wanted to return, for they intended to make a complete break with Cornwall. And they could afford to do so, for they were not poor. They had land to sell and enough money to buy land in Wisconsin at the going rate of $1.25 an acre. They did not even need the inducement of free land.[3] They were well educated (Samuel may even have attended the local grammar school at Helston whose headmaster in 1827 was Derwent Coleridge, the son of the poet), well-read, well informed about local and national affairs, and radical in their politics and religion. What he and his wife were looking for in Wisconsin, as he said in a letter to his brother-in-law, was a country where he could bring up his family without the risk of being involved in a war, where industriousness brought its own rewards, and where he could be useful even to the point of helping others to emigrate. In ringing words he exclaimed that he wanted 'to go where the light of heaven, the vital air, the fish of the sea and the produce of the earth, necessary for the sustenance of men, are free for all as intended by their Creator'.

There can be little doubt about the quality of the idealism that fundamentally motivated Samuel. It might be described as utilitarianism strengthened by a belief in the perfectibility of man, that man is by nature good and that it is the institutions that make him bad, a blend of Rosseau, Bentham and Godwin. All the ingredients are here to explain why he believed that there was still a Golden Age to inherit and it could be found in the young United States which had thrown off the so-called civilisation of Europe. We know that he found Wisconsin disappointing and that he returned to Cornwall for a year and found that disappointing too, but how else are we to explain his decision to leave Wisconsin when he and his wife were 46 and 45 years old, with a young family to bring up and brave the Oregon Trail? It also meant leaving a settled, comfortable and compact Cornish community with excellent farming prospects and that Anna

Maria would never see her mother or brothers and sisters again. All their relatives must have thought that the Oregon venture was foolhardy and quite unnecessary. One suspects that Samuel found in Wisconsin the same dead hand of church and state institutions as in Cornwall, and that he felt he must once more begin life all over again. The same pattern would happen again in both Oregon and Washington Territory.

The decision to build another future in Oregon called for special qualities of leadership, for survival on the trail depended on skills of improvisation, self-reliance, resourcefulness, an ability to read the 'signs' of the landscape, and ultimately a belief in one's inner strength to endure the discomforts of the body. All these qualities Samuel possessed but they had not yet been tested in the fire of trail experience. He was deliberately turning his back on 'civilisation', though in carrying his library of books with him he was introducing into the wilderness some of the best expressions of that civilisation. In a way Samuel conforms to the pattern of the new American who opened up the West before the new emigrants streamed in from Europe later in the nineteenth century, the educated man of books who is also the practical man, the reader of Milton's poems who was also expert in the use of the bowie knife.

The move onwards from Wisconsin called for the most careful planning, waiting for the right year, even spending a winter at Dudley, some four hundred miles along the trail, to facilitate an early start in the Spring. To his Cornish experience he had added much he learned in Wisconsin from ordinary uneducated men, how to fell trees and to persuade oxen to pull wagons, and discovered how necessary it was to cast aside old habits and methods and adapt to new conditions. But Samuel could hardly have succeeded without the whole-hearted support of his wife, Anna Maria. She was as much a pioneer as he was, and in some ways more so, for much was expected from women on the trail. Remarkably well-educated and liberated, she was gay, vivacious, disciplined and a model of cheerfulness, as well as being a much loved mother. She must have been completely in agreement with Samuel's views to have sacrificed the comforts of home and the loss of relatives for the discomforts of the trail and the prospects of building a life in a wilderness where they knew no one.

The prospects for Anna Maria were daunting. Women on the trail usually rose at 4 a.m. before the men, built the fires, boiled the water, milked the cattle, fixed breakfast, while at night-fall they carried water, cooked dinner, washed dishes, made beds, cleaned out wagons, checked the provisions, mended clothes, and washed children. During the day's travel they were expected to keep an eye open for suitable camp sites, gather fuel, on occasion to drive the oxen and always to watch that the children did not stray. In addition they nursed the sick and there were plenty of illnesses to contend with: gastro-enteritis, mountain fever, splitting headaches, pains in muscles and joints, prolonged chills, mosquito and rattlesnake bites, and horrifying deaths when in a moment of carelessness in stepping down from a moving wagon a traveller would be crushed under the wheels. In these matters Anna Maria had to be more of a learner than her husband, for the guide books hardly ever catered for the women's problems. The only way to learn was to mingle with other women, and the only day to do that was on the Sabbath. It was the women who insisted that the Sabbath must be a rest day so that they could reduce the physical and emotional stress under which they were compelled to solve their problems. Yet there is hardly a mention of these troubles in Samuel's log-book, proof that his careful planning left nothing to chance.[4]

After the failure to find suitable land in Oregon, it was in Washington Territory, not yet a state (that was not to come until 1889), that Samuel and Anna Maria put their ideas and skills into practice. It was an untamed prairie and John Rogers said that a great fear came over them when they realised they had brought their family into a wilderness where not even the wild animals were afraid of them. They were the only inhabitants apart from a few Indians and they were among the very first white people the Indians had ever seen. And in their first winter Cornish and Indian shared a common grief when one of the James children died and he was buried within sight of their cabin between 'three towering fir trees' as John Rogers described the moving scene, with the Indians present.

It was there that Samuel proved his worth as backwoodsman, frontier farmer, and father of a family of pioneers, young men and girls alike. They first had to fell oaks and maple, fir and cedar, split the wood and then build their first cabin. Furniture had to be made by hand, cedar shakes (tiles) for the roof, and fencing to keep in the cattle. They began sheep farming, planted grain, and helped the Indians to deal with the scourge of smallpox. As new settlers arrived, Samuel started a church, and a Sunday School, and helped the new arrivals to file applications for grants of land. He organised prayer meetings in neighbours' houses and 'camp meetings' at Scatter Creek with guest speakers like George Whitworth.

But the new settlers, mainly from the eastern states, brought with them the bickering and bitterness associated with politics and organised religion. So Samuel and Anna Maria decided it was time again to move even further west. They had a feeling of being over-crowded, especially as there was little government land left for sale. Samuel wanted new land where he could expand his family's stock of beef cattle and sheep, and he found it overlooking the Pacific Ocean at Grays Harbor, where he bought 160 acres. Here he built a second home, the wood freighted down the Chehalis River on a home-made raft which became the foundations of the house, again planted acres of fruit trees, fenced in the tidal prairie for new herds, and supplied mutton and beef to the markets of Victoria by boat shipment through Olympia. And it was here that he suffered his fatal stroke.

The last twenty-five years of Samuel's life had been momentous, eventful and strangely exhilarating. Undoubtedly he and his family have their place in the settlement of a remote corner of the Pacific North-West of the United States. The frontier was pushed further and further westwards by fur traders, cattlemen and miners, but above all by successive waves of farmers who were skilled in wresting a living from the soil, who knew how to clear land, build a home, fence fields, erect a defence system and plant crops, as well as rear cattle and sheep. Throughout the history of American westward expansion the farmer, blessed with wealth and skills, was the true frontiersman. As the American historian, Ray Billington, observes in the classic *Westward Expansion, A History of the American Frontier* (p. 11): 'But the true hero of the tale was the hard-working farmer who, axe in hand, marched ever westward until the boundaries of the nation touched the Pacific.' And among these heroes can be counted Samuel James, by origin a Celt from Cornwall, by choice, inclination and hard experience an American.

The Cornish legacy left at Grand Mound by Samuel and Anna Maria, says David James, was their children and their large families. Samuel, the eldest, William, Thomas and John Rogers, all born in Cornwall, were 17, 15, 13 and 11 years old when the overland journey began. Samuel junior, nervous and easily worried, produced a daughter and six sons, was an outstanding Grand Mound farmer, was four times elected an assessor of taxes for Thurston County, and died in 1906 at the age of 72. William his brother, like his father, was handy with tools and at managing livestock, but never married and died in 1871. In the same year died Thomas, something of the scholar like his father and successful in merchandising in Victoria in British Columbia. John Rogers fathered four sons and five daughters, was in ranching, business ventures and property development and enjoyed a reputation as a historian of the Oregon Trail. He outlived them all and died in 1929 at the age of 89. The last son, Richard Oregon, born in Wisconsin, died, still a bachelor, in 1907. The two daughters of Samuel and Anna Maria, Ann Elizabeth and Mary Ann Frances each bore three children.[5] So there were 22 grandchildren, all of them at Grand Mound locked in the community known as 'Jamestown'.

The Cornish connection has never really been forgotten. In 1952 the first centenary of the Jameses' settling in Washington Territory was celebrated by a family reunion at Grand Mound which attracted almost two hundred descendants and their friends. Another anniversary, the 125th, was observed in 1977 and even more descendants and friends participated. But more remarkable is that, in the early 1900s, annual gatherings began to take place and continue to this day. The first Sunday in August is always set aside by the family to meet at Grand Mound and to rejoice in the traditions made possible by Samuel and his wife. And from Cornwall and the United States the James family has expanded outwards to include wives and husbands from Sweden, Norway, Denmark, Germany, Italy, Finland, Ireland, Scotland, England, France and Belgium. And the inclusion of other nations continues, a 'one world for all' in which Samuel James believed.

NOTES

1. David James, *From Grand Mound to Scatter Creek*, p. 7.
2. See Alfred O. Dray, *Not by Might: the story of Whitworth College 1890–1965*, Whitworth College, Spokane, Washington, 1965.
3. John Rogers James in his autobiography revealed that his father, when the sale of his property in Cornwall was still incomplete and he was considering moving from Wisconsin to Oregon, told his solicitor in Helston, a Mr Edwards, not to send him any more money as he had plenty. Samuel instructed Edwards to use the money from the sale of this property to set up a fund to pay every three months 'this or that old man or woman who had been one of his tenants or workmen . . . [which] kept several old people away from the poor house'. When Samuel died in 1866 there was still £2,000 left in the fund, which was paid to his widow.
4. See Sharon A. Brown, 'Women on the Overland Trails—A Historical Perspective', *Overland Journal*, Oregon-California Trails Association, Vol. 2, No. 1, Winter 1984 pp. 35–38; and Peter D. Olch, 'Treading The Elephant's Tail: Medical Problems on the Overland Trails', *Bulletin of the History of Medicine*, Vol. 59, 1985, Yale University, New Haven, Connecticut, pp. 196–212.
5. Mary Ann Frances James married a Methodist preacher, Charles Shephard, and died in 1913 in her 65th year. One of her daughters, Margory, married an English seaman named Turner and lived in the north of England. When he died he left enough money to the Royal National Lifeboat Institution to buy an Atlantic 21 lifeboat, which is permanently stationed at Youghal on the south coast of Eire. It bears the name of Samuel's grand-daughter, 'Margory Turner'.

INDEX